CONCILIUM
Religion in the Seventies

CONCILIUM

New Series: Volume 3, Number 10: Dogma

JESUS CHRIST AND HUMAN FREEDOM

Edited by
Edward Schillebeeckx and Bas van Iersel

Herder and Herder

1974
HERDER AND HERDER NEW YORK
815 Second Avenue
New York 10017

ISBN: 0-8164-2577-9

Library of Congress Catalog Card Number: 73-17908
Copyright © 1974 by McGraw-Hill Inc. and Stichting Concilium

Printed in the United States

Contents

PART II
DOCUMENTATION

Editorial

"FREEDOM" and "liberation" have become evocative words today and they have an important function, although "freedom" has tended to be more significant in the past. The contemporary importance of "liberation", however, has given new meaning to "freedom". The classical definitions of freedom are therefore no longer entirely applicable to the modern situation.

Aristotle defined freedom as man's autonomous self-determination to good or evil. According to Augustine, the word could only be used in the sense of freedom to do good, since freedom to act evilly was not freedom. Thomas Aquinas tried to synthesize both these views. None of these definitions can be applied without reservation to our understanding of freedom today, because our experience of freedom is different and we are confronted with new problems.

The main problem today is that of the dialectical relationship between the inner liberation of man himself (his conversion or change of heart) and his liberation from structural violence. This has obvious consequences for the question of the relationship between the social processes and personal emancipation on the one hand and Christian freedom on the other. It has moreover consequences for the way in which Jesus is expressed by theologians and non-theologians both inside and outside the Christian churches. In other words, it has consequences for christology.

This issue of *Concilium* is above all a contribution to a new christology with something meaningful to say about Jesus at a time when people are deeply stirred by the concept of liberation.

The precise meaning of "freedom" and "liberation" in this christological investigation will emerge in the articles in this issue. In this editorial, we must be content to formulate the questions that we have asked of the various contributors in the hope that the reader will thereby gain a deeper insight into the way in which the articles and documentations are interconnected.

I. Yes to Jesus—No to God and the Church

Christian Duquoc was asked whether the impression that we have nowadays that more and more people are saying "yes" to Jesus, but "no" to God and the Church is a correct one and whether he could describe the problem and provide an analysis of the situation which might form a background to the later articles in this issue. Any description of this problem leads inevitably to further questions, such as, is it true that those who want to preserve the *status quo* appeal to an "unchanging" God, whereas those who want to change society are more concerned with "Jesus of Nazareth"? If this is true, why is it so? What idea of God lies behind it? What is the relationship between this idea of God and that presented by the Bible? Is it possible to contrast Jesus and God in this way? Are people right to reject the Church because it contains an inner contradiction which is expressed in faith both in the Father, as the symbol of stability and authority, and in the Son, as the symbol of revolt and progress?

Going a stage further, we may ask also about the possibility of speaking about a universal significance of Jesus against the background of a description of the contemporary situation. What meaning can this really have? Can a non-theistic view of Jesus, a Jewish concept of Christ or religious faith in him which is not bound to Church membership or which is opposed to the Church be justified and valid? What can the churches say to these people about Christ? Why do non-Christians oppose the universal significance ascribed by the churches to Jesus? Do they feel that they have been wrongly annexed by Christianity?

On the other hand, how can we prevent Jesus, isolated from God and separated from the Church, from becoming an empty symbol, a mere cipher in man's expectations, utopias and ideologies, and from being filled with any content and thus losing all his real meaning.

Finally, do we do full justice to Jesus when we speak about him in terms of freedom and liberation? Has this anything at all to do with what has always been known in Christian theology as redemption? Can the figure of Jesus be used as a criticism of the contemporary concepts, freedom and liberation?

II. Is the Promotion of Freedom a Monopoly of Jesus or Christianity?

If Christians believe that Jesus has a universal significance and an essential place in the history of man's freedom, there is a danger that this will lead to their claiming that only Jesus has brought about true freedom. This monopoly can then be extended to the churches, which scandalizes many people. We therefore asked Josef Neuner to examine whether this claim was justified.

It is, of course, quite clear that there are many sources of freedom and many means of liberation—science, technology, art, work, psychoanalysis, andragogy, freedom movements, and so on. The fact that these all promote unfreedom does not mean that they are not at the same time also potential sources of freedom and liberation.

The same applies to the various religions of the world. Values such as freedom, liberation and redemption all play an important part in every religious system, although the real significance of these religions for human freedom is open to discussion. Many people believe, however, that religion makes man unfree and that freedom from religion is therefore an essential part of the process of emancipation.

What are we to think about the Christian monopoly of freedom and liberation against this background? And what is the authentic and irreducible contribution that Jesus can make to the history of man's freedom? Has the freedom which can provide men with civilization, science, technology, and so on, clear boundaries and is that freedom (and its possible boundaries) different from the freedom for which the different religions strive, the freedom which Jesus has brought about and which the Christian churches claim to serve? If these two freedoms are different, what is the relationship between them?

III. The Freedom brought about by Jesus

We cannot speak about Jesus and human freedom without considering what the New Testament has to say about them. Three authors were therefore asked to approach this question from different points of view.

First of all, a daunting obstacle has to be cleared out of the way. The way in which the question of the "historical Jesus" has been discussed has made many people despair of being able to say anything convincing about Jesus. This despair is, of course, much greater than it should be in view of recent developments in New Testament studies. For this reason, we asked Dieter Lührmann to investigate the possibility of bridging the gap between the "historical Jesus" and the "kerygmatic Christ", using the category of "memory" if he thought fit. He has in fact gone into this question in some detail, discussing the effect that our memory of Jesus' words and deeds may have on the process of liberation.

This is not the only obstacle, however. Many Christians used to believe, and may still believe, that Jesus was not free, like other men, to do what he wanted to do, but that he was so to speak "pre-programmed". This may be because of the one-sided emphasis of what has been called a "christology from above", in which Jesus was regarded as the Son of God who had come down from heaven and who lived, thought and acted entirely from his essential unity with God. It may also have been encouraged by the emphasis that has been until recently placed on New Testament themes such as "carrying out the will of God", obedience to the Father", and so on. This in turn gives rise to the question as to the relationship between these themes and the stories and statements in the gospels which show Jesus as the man who liberated men from the power of demons and brought them to themselves by the power of God's Spirit. Rudolf Pesch has made quite clear in his contribution the sense in which Jesus has to be called a free man and how his own freedom was a source of freedom for others.

In the third of these articles, Leander Keck has approached this question from another standpoint. The word "freedom" does not occur in the synoptic gospels and "free" occurs only once. Both are, however, key-words in Paul's writings and there is at least one important passage in the fourth gospel in which they play a leading part. It seemed valuable therefore to examine the significance of Jesus for human freedom in Paul and John and in this way to review the synoptics in the expectation that important christological questions would come to light.

Examples of the questions that arise in this context are: From what and to what end does Jesus make men free? What is the relationship between this freedom and the kingdom of God? What is the relationship between Jesus' words and deeds in this context and his own person? Does his liberating action also mean that he rejects a certain image of God and certain ways in which men come together? What is the essence of Jesus' liberation? Is there any connection between Paul's fight for freedom from the Torah and Jesus' own person? What are the implications of all this for the community of believers?

IV. THE PRICE OF FREEDOM

Midway between biblical and dogmatic theology is the systematic study of the function of biblical words and word systems. This is to some extent present in the article entitled "The Price of Freedom". Jesus' freedom and liberating activity cost him dearly, since he bought the freedom which he gained for others with his own blood. In the New Testament, as in the preceding sentence, this is often discussed in the language of trade, debt, paying, buying, redeeming, the ransoming of slaves, and so on. In this context, the word "freedom" has a very concrete meaning, although it is, of course, used in a figurative sense. The best approach to this question is through a theological analysis which is similar in its method to the science of linguistics and is therefore often known as "linguistic" theology.

One of the representatives of this theology, Walter Magass, was therefore asked to write this article, in which he has extended the language of trade to include barter, exchange, giving and taking, and so on, and from there to the idea of taking, distributing, giving and eating and the community at table. He uses this finally to throw light on freedom and liberation.

This also provided us with the opportunity to introduce this new branch of theology to those readers who were still unacquainted with it. It is far from easy, but that is something that must be accepted in any new study. On the other hand, it is also up to the "linguistic" theologians themselves to determine what price the reader is prepared to pay for what degree of difficulty.

V. THE CHURCH AS THE PLACE OF FREEDOM

If freedom and liberation were in fact essentially important to Jesus, the Church cannot be indifferent to human freedom and movements of liberation. None the less, according to many people, the Church is not the place of freedom, but rather a place of unfreedom, because, for all that it may say about freedom, it does very little.

The questions arising within this context, then, are, for example: What is the relationship between speaking about and bringing about freedom? What is specifically Christian freedom, as compared with human freedom? In what sense can the Church be the place of freedom? What kind of freedom is the Church concerned with? If the Church lives in and for the memory of the freedom that Jesus brought about, what kind of memory is that? Is it a theoretical or a practical memory or is it a combination of both? If it is a combination of the two, how are theory and practice related to each other? What should be the attitude of the Church towards the freedom movements of today? What position should it take between the forces that claim to be striving to change society and bring about freedom and the other forces that claim to be protecting freedom by preserving the *status quo*? These and similar questions were put to Nicholas Lash, who, in his article, set them in order, examined how they were interrelated and attempted to find an answer.

VI. THE GOD OF JESUS AND THE JESUS OF GOD

Edward Schillebeeckx has tried, in his contribution, to complete the series of articles in this issue by providing a thematic and dogmatic discussion of the position of Jesus and God. We are, as men living in a world where many claim to be "liberators" and to make an active contribution to human freedom, confronted with the question: What can the Jesus in whom we believe contribute to this freedom? To what extent can we say "There is salvation in no one else" (Acts 4. 12)?

This question arises in an acute form in the light of Jesus' apparent failure which became visible in his execution. Has his name not become an empty symbol, a "cipher" which has to be filled again and again with a new content?

There are countless other questions which are asked in this context. Can we really speak about Jesus without speaking about God? Can we discuss God without narrating the history of Jesus? What is the best kind of language that the theologian, who aims to speak about Jesus and his significance for the freedom and liberation of men and human institutions, can choose? Is it the language of systematic thought, theoretical concepts, analysis and definition? Or should it be the language of theology? Are there perhaps others who can understand and use this language better?

VII.   The Documentation

The three contributions to the documentation of this issue of *Concilium* do not form part of this plan, but they are related to the subject in general. In a sense, they look beyond the rather narrow confines of the plan itself.

It is obviously unnecessary to justify Gerhard Adler's contribution on the Jesus People and the churches, in which he discusses above all the message that this movement has for the churches. The issue concludes with two contributions on the so-called theology of liberation, which clearly goes beyond the frontiers of traditional theology. Initially, only one contribution was planned on this subject, but, because of an error, two were submitted. They are, however, by good fortune complementary and can both be included because the other articles in this issue are mostly quite short. It is, moreover, excellent to be able to include two Latin American contributions, because the theology of that sub-continent is still too little known in the countries in which *Concilium* for the most part appears.

BAS VAN IERSEL
EDWARD SCHILLEBEECKX

PART I
ARTICLES

Christian Duquoc

Yes to Jesus—No to God and the Church

THE results of various surveys recently made in France on the subject of the religious convictions of the French do not endorse the opinion stated in our title. On the contrary, they show that belief in God has more popular support than faith in Jesus Christ. A recently published book[1] confirms the findings of these surveys. It is called "Does God exist?—No!" and, although many of the intellectuals interviewed answer "no" with varying shades of conviction, it would be a mistake to read into their agnostic answers a leaning towards faith in Jesus Christ. Indeed the God who is impugned by many of them is not the metaphysical God, that is to say the omnipotent, omniscient, unchanging, impassive God who caused the world, but the personal God who is involved in the movement of our history. In reading the interviews, the Christian is surprised by the strength of the old arguments, such as that of evil in the world and the indifference to the new evidence, such as the much-vaunted recession in religious conviction so often used by Christian sociologists to describe the absence of God. So we see that a debate presented in terms of an opposition between Jesus and God is proving to be a debate between Christians. It expresses the repulsion some of them feel at the possibility of reaching God other than through revelation in Jesus. Yet Chabanis's investigation does show a certain awareness of this opposition. The refusal to admit that God has a personal character, the

[1] J. Chabanis, *Dieu existe-t-il ? Non* (Paris, 1973).

acceptance by several of those interviewed of some kind of divinity and the recognition of their incapacity to resolve the question of the first cause are, in their view, consequences of the scandal produced by the simultaneity of a rigorously intelligible world order and the harshness of the cosmic laws. Some of them see the world as unthinkable without a thought that thinks it, yet incoherent for a personal will to have created it out of goodness. Thus the God of metaphysics is simultaneously affirmed and denied. Does this not postulate another God, the God of Jesus Christ? In fact the God of Jesus seems to many agnostics even less acceptable, because he corresponds to the movement of desire rather than to that of intelligence. We are thus confined to a debate between believers, while hoping that the crisis within the Christian community may also have some significance for non-Christians.

But non-Christians may also be religious. International communications have shown how alive the non-Christian religions still are today. God is sought and honoured by those who believe in them, but they cannot accept that God could have involved himself once and for all in a single historical figure, Jesus. It would be dangerous to confine ourselves to a debate between Christians without realizing that the rejection of Christianity by believers is not always due to its Western label but to the fact that they sense an incongruity in its historicity and particularity regarding the destiny of God himself. It is therefore in this perspective that I shall study the phenomenon specific to the churches, namely adherence to Jesus and rejection of God and the Church. For it is in the context of agnosticism and non-Christian belief that we should, as I see it, examine this opposition. I shall start by outlining the forms of adherence to Jesus and rejection of God and the Church. I shall then suggest motivations. Finally, I shall assess the changes in Christian awareness with regard to the questions presented by agnosticism and the non-Christian religions.

I. ADHERENCE TO JESUS AND REJECTION OF GOD AND THE CHURCH

The secular theologies and the theologies of the "death of God" have been instrumental in bringing out the opposition between Jesus and God. These theologians have attacked the doctrine of God represented as omnipotent, eternal, impassive, unchanging and self-sufficient in himself and independent of any link with the world. They are hostile to the most widely held images of God which are, moreover, often supported by the official documents of the churches. Their two main reasons for criticizing these images of God are, on the one hand, the need to save Christian faith from being swept along by metaphysics and, on the other, the conviction that there is no common ground between adherence to Jesus Christ and belief in a metaphysical God.

The need to find a new basis for Christian faith has played a large part. The secular and the "death of God" theologians have been struck by the recession of religious conviction. They have been impressed by the findings of the sociological surveys. But these things have not caused them to despair of the future of Christianity. Paradoxically enough, they have even detected an opportunity for faith in the phenomenon so deplored by the hierarchies of the churches. As they see it, faith would finally come into its own if only it were stripped of the dubious props of Western tradition and Greek metaphysics. So the disappearance of metaphysical supports of the doctrine traditionally taught in the churches seemed to these theologians a positive symptom of the contemporary renewal of faith.

One of the principal tasks these theologians then set themselves was to discover a concrete support suitable to the needs imposed by the evolution of our culture. In their view the structure of Christianity provided them with it. It proclaims Jesus, Saviour and Messiah. It was easy to show that these two qualifications enrolled him in the rank of liberators; and in another connection there was no difficulty in establishing that his divinization in accordance with a metaphysical model had been the product of a cultural reinterpretation. Christianity was too daring (so the argument goes) to have been understood from its very beginning—the transformation of the image of God that it brought about was not grasped. On the contrary, it was the dominant image, with metaphysical orientations, that transformed Christianity through making its founder, Jesus, acceptable. Jesus was then torn from his concrete historical setting and so became an illustration of the metaphysical attributes of God.

The cultural situation has evolved since then. The image is no longer one of an omnipotent and unchanging God governing the progress of the world from within the indifference of his own happiness. The dominant image is that of a history produced by man and for which man is responsible. He himself is the creator of his values, he no longer receives them from previous laws. For a long time it seemed easy enough to harmonize the Jesus of the gospels with the image of the metaphysical God—but the harmonization was achieved at the price of a certain selectivity: thus the human aspects of Jesus were passed over in silence and the superhuman ones exaggerated, his actual history was forgotten and only his universal example persisted. It was the resurrection that permitted this harmonization or transfer operation, of reconciling the Galilean's attitudes with the immutability and impassivity of the metaphysical monotheism at that time prevailing in the Mediterranean basin.

I do not claim that the reinterpretation took place in this way historically, but I do think that the Christian affirmation of God was often lived in this way in the churches. Hence the justification for the criticisms made by the secular theologians and those of the "death of God". Indeed if these two groups of theologians differ in their views on secularization, they are in agreement in their rejection of the metaphysical God and their adherence to Jesus. And they are no less agreed in their hostility to the institutional churches, which, they believe, have betrayed the gospel message through shifting its centre of gravity from the figure of the liberating Jesus to the conservative symbol of divine fatherhood. Instead of highlighting the freedom proclaimed by Jesus, the churches have fought against the originality of the Christian message and manipulated the religious instinct. As far as these theologians are concerned, God and the Church are both rejected for the same reason—the betrayal of the gospel in favour of metaphysics and a betrayal with social and psychological bases.

However, we must not overestimate the influence of these theologies. Whatever their merits may be, they are symptoms of a malaise within the Christian consciousness rather than rigorously thought-out systems. In fact the convictions or intuitions from which they have been elaborated are the property of people who have never had either the opportunity or the desire to read them. The "Jesus movement" in the United States is a phenomenon having no common ground with theological thinking about secularization. In first analysis it seems opposed to the intuitions of the secular theologies. Yet we nevertheless have to admit that there are close fundamental convictions between these theologies and the movement in question. Similarly the options that underlie certain manifestoes of Catholic Action movements in France—those that unite believers in an association such as "Lettre", or those that inspire Christians interested in basic communities to meet, for example, at Boquen—prove the extent to which the figure of Jesus has assumed importance for Christian faith at the very moment when contestation was flaring up in the churches and metaphysical certainties were floundering. We are witnessing a veritable reversal of the traditional religious order. The figure of Christ used not to play a primordial role. The dominant symbol used to be that of the omnipotent God, scrutineer and judge, no doubt proclaimed as good but felt to be threatening and remote. This relationship with God was not in accordance with the mediation of Jesus. Hence popular traditional Christianity conferred on Mary the qualities which, in theological elaboration, belonged by rights to Christ. This organization of the relationship with God is in process of transformation, as is evidenced by the facts we have quoted, but, as is shown by the theologies mentioned above and as Freud has already pointed out, where Jesus takes first place he eliminates God's place. This, it seems to me, is the path that has been trodden by countless believers, with varying degrees of coherence. We must now try to show the reasons for this transformation.

II. The Reasons for Adherence to Jesus and Rejection of God and the Church

The reasons that I suggest for this transformation are very tentative. Interpretations of the transformation are certainly not lacking. Many have been proposed by the secular and "death of

God" theologies, though they are not identical with the more political interpretations emanating from marginal Christians. To make myself plain, here I am discussing the interpretations of the secular theologies and marginal groups. It is within the context of these two movements that I shall describe the part played by Jesus in the current rejection of God and the Church.

The secular theologies and those of the "death of God" are theologies of freedom. Without fear of error, we can say that they have introduced into Christianity thoughts that were familiar to the philosophers of the eighteenth century. The secular theologians are aware of the modern movement towards emancipation where the processes of power are concerned. For them the Church represents the quintessence of authority because it justifies its social role and its privileges in the order of knowledge of morality through the authority of God. The decline of its cultural and political influence was accompanied by an increase in civic and individual freedoms. And it is also observable that the claims of science came into force when confessional and authoritarian theology was on the decline. Civic, moral and political responsibilities increased as clerical power diminished. All these forms of emancipation from immature dependence on the churches had an effect on the validity of the ideology which lay at the root of their power, namely, the metaphysical God. According to these theologians, man had been robbed of his public and private freedoms because order had been defined once and for all by a philosophy of being whose principle was God, and man had no choice but to submit. Moreover, the traditional attributes of God—his omnipotent, unchangeable, eternal character—were taken over as if by osmosis by the institution that had assumed the task of witnessing to the metaphysical order of the world and of upholding its social function. To rob the ecclesiastical institution of its effective power was to deprive of credibility the metaphysical ideology that guaranteed it. The socio-political transformation of the West gradually stripped the Church of its social influence, and thenceforward its ideology too became redundant. If the Church must still witness to something, it should no longer be to the metaphysical order, whose common name is God, because that order has disappeared. It must witness to the figure from whom it received the name of Christian and whom it had forgotten, Jesus.

The critical attitude of the marginal groups is fairly close to the one I have just outlined, though it puts stronger emphasis on the political reasons for its adherence to Jesus and its rejection of God and the Church. Indeed these groups see in the upholding of an unchanging, impassive and omniscient God the philosophical and religious buttress of a natural law which forms the basis of economics, politics and morality. Many facts in the Church's recent history seem to support the truth of this judgment. In the last century Bastiat considered it senseless to fight against the liberal regime of economic competition. To attack it, that is to say to dispute the laws of the market, was to blaspheme against the order established by Providence. Marx chose to be such a blasphemer, claiming that the laws of the market were not divine, but the creation of man, and what man had made he could unmake. I could quote no less surprising examples dating from a more recent epoch. The churches' antagonistic attitude towards socialism can be explained by its hostility to a transformation of society as much as by theological reasons. These are not to be ignored, however, as they provide an ideology that justifies a state of things that is endangered by the very social contradictions it engenders.

The accusations brought against the metaphysical image of God spring from this image's socio-political function. So we can well understand that Christians who want to weight their faith in favour of a socialist transformation of society choose other images as their point of reference, notably that of a liberating or contestatory Jesus. Jesus was indeed a free man, he ratified neither the established religion nor the existing political system. He fought against the ideology of the Pharisees and attacked the power of the Saducean priests. He was an unsparing moral teacher, made himself the neighbour of those rejected by society and was not afraid to let himself be proclaimed a prophet by the poor and the oppressed. He certainly talked about God and called him his Father, but the God he talked about is in no way comparable with the metaphysical image subsequently bestowed on him by the churches. Far from being impassive and unchanging, the God of Jesus rejoices when the lost sheep is found, when the impoverished son returns, when the sinner is forgiven. In his preaching, the old God is dead. As for the image of the Church which mediates Jesus' message, it is that of a free community of brothers, breaking with cultural and moral obligations, tolerant towards diversity of conviction. Jesus imposes no confession of faith on the centurion or the woman of Cana.

In their desire to bring freer and more brotherly communities to birth, the contestatory and marginal groups are expressing a hope and an uneasiness shared by many believers. They hope that the opposition between the open face of Jesus and the present reality of the Church, resented by many, will disappear. They are uneasy because the affirmation of the hope proclaimed by the gospel seems to involve excluding what has been transmitted by the Church for so long, so that it is not without reservations that we have to break the image of a Father-God, symbol of authority and stability, to turn towards Jesus, the brother, symbol of progress, revolt and freedom. Many Christians hesitate to commit themselves to this revolutionary path. Will the Christian community be able, without a definitive split, to accept this transference from a religion of authority to a religion of freedom? If the "yes to Jesus" represents the future of Christianity—as it seems to for many—there is a temptation to take refuge in and to recover assurance among the old symbols of the fatherhood of God and the motherhood of the Church. Few people seem decided to take literally Jesus' words: "Anyone who loves his father or mother more than me is not worthy of me" (Matt. 10. 37) as applied to a departure far from the traditional family household that the Church has for so long represented.

To sum up, we may say that the causes for defection from the metaphysical God and the institutional Church fall into two types. On the one hand, there are those that correspond to the unconsciously apologetic tendencies of the secular theologies and integrate with the Christian faith the movement springing from the conquests of political and cultural autonomy in the modern world. On the other hand, there are those that arise from a will to political struggle against the social organization deriving from capitalism, and discern in religious manifestations of high metaphysical density an ideology that works in favour of the established order. These various causes highlight the figure of Jesus as a free and contestatory man. They are directed towards the historical face of Jesus rather than towards the Lord of glory and indeed the secular theologians look to the gospel for concrete props for their struggle against the dominant images and for their revolt against ecclesiastical organization. This transformation of the normal poles of Christian practice—the substitution of a contestatory founder for an unchangeable God—presents theological problems about the validity of the opposition between Jesus and God, not only in its content but even in its revolutionary function.

III. Yes to Jesus, Agnosticism and the Non-Christian Religions

Adherence to Jesus with rejection of God and the Church presents problems that cannot be treated lightly. At the beginning of this article I outlined briefly the allergy felt by many believers for the over-historical character of Christianity: they view it as absurd that God should have linked his destiny with that of a first-century Jew. Yet adherence to Jesus outside all theist frames of reference makes the privilege accorded to this man more difficult to understand. If, on the one hand, the trust we place in him means nothing more than a recognition of the value and hence the possible universality of his message, Jesus is no more than a sage and a thinker like other sages and thinkers. His teaching has simply to be assessed by its capacity to enable men to live together and give meaning to their lives and his personality disappears behind his message. If, on the other hand, he is a heroic model who, in a particularly exemplary situation of conflict, was faithful to death to the liberating task he had set himself, Jesus is then similar to a revolutionary hero like Che Guevara. But in that case our interest in him stems from the weight of Western tradition which has singled him out from among all possible heroes and we are still prisoners of this tradition. So if there is no theist frame of reference it seems to me vain to try to justify the privilege accorded to Jesus —a privilege that postulates in effect that there is no other name in which we can be saved (Acts 4. 12). This means that all men should put their faith in Jesus.

In reality, the "theist" frame of reference is present in the "yes" to Jesus, but in another way. The rejected God is the God described as "metaphysical". The rejection of this God for historical or political reasons conceals a more deeply-rooted intuition. If we take Jesus' position seriously as the final determinant of the Christian's faith, then we cannot simultaneously accept the image of God as mediated by the so-called metaphysical tradition upheld so strongly by the churches. Thus it is important for us to show that God is certainly other than the God who is constantly put before us, but that we cannot in fact state anything about this God outside his manifestation in Jesus.

This rarely-mentioned intuition is confirmed by a counterproof. Those of our Christian contemporaries who still cling to a metaphysical theology of Platonic inspiration show very great uneasiness with regard to Jesus. They do not know where to place him and see a contradiction between the unique historical character of Jesus and the manifestation of the Absolute. The theist framework within which the figure of Jesus can be placed is a specific theist framework, for the intuition of adherence to Jesus within the rejection of God (bringing in its wake the rejection of a Church seen as unfaithful to the gospel) postulates that the image of God cannot precede the perception of Jesus' attitudes but must follow it. This is, however, rarely made clear, with the result that adherence to Jesus seems to be satisfied with opposing the dominant image of God on the grounds that it plays a retrogressive social function. Yet the framework would have to be made very explicit if we wish to maintain Jesus' universality.

By Jesus' universality we mean the conviction that his existence, his attitude and his transmitted words touch all men in the definition of their destiny. Those who adhere to Jesus while rejecting God do not challenge this perspective. However, if they fail to integrate this privilege of Jesus within a theist framework, they are in danger of making the claim of Christianity still more difficult for agnostics and non-Christian believers to understand. Indeed for agnostics such a Christian claim will represent at best the sum of human hopes of liberation or the utopia of a brotherly society. But then they will wonder why we have to jump back twenty centuries so as to take our rules of action from a first-century Palestinian. Still less will they see why the movements that say "yes" to Jesus for political motives should show a huge indifference regarding the most common laws of the exegesis, and should dare to saddle this "Palestinian" with ideas that emerged only long after his death.

Recourse to Jesus outside all theist frame of reference will therefore seem either symbolical or mythical. It will be symbolical because it indicates that no political and cultural movement of the present time possesses the energy and amplitude of what was born from Jesus' words and attitudes, and that the gospel is still the vital spring in our contemporary bankruptcy. It will otherwise be mythical because Jesus is the geometric point of all dreams and utopias. He is historical and cultural exoticism. For those who are tired of the drab materialism of our technical and scientific societies, he represents the distant dream of freedom without shackles and brotherhood without problems. He is the "innocent" described by Wilhelm Reich in his book *The Murder of Christ*. But whatever the grandeur of this dream, it cannot satisfy the really searching spirit. It is also by no means certain that its adherents' denunciation of the retrogressive social function of the dominant image of God does not redound against their representation of Jesus. After all, as the sum total of all our dreams, he represents no reality that we can confront, he structures nothing and he justifies the desire to flee from a world so deeply beset with soul-sickness.

Nor is this image of Jesus acceptable to non-Christian believers. These are religious people for whom the encounter with the Absolute is not an empty expression, it is not something that happens in dreams. In the ancient texts the Absolute is not at our command to be manipulated as we will. On the contrary, progress towards the Absolute is marked out by rules, methods and religious acts—a progress thought out by Islamic mystics, by believers in Hinduism, or by the Buddhists, whose thought represents the peak of negative theology, like a progress into the night. To reduce the Absolute to a man, hero though he may be, is to practise idolatry. To draw Jesus within a theist framework is to make the Christian claim to universality even less acceptable, because despite the declared desacralization, something is being sacralized that should never be sacralized— a man. To substitute Jesus for God is to blaspheme. The attempt to de-structure Christianity from the metaphysical point of view brings with it the danger of ignoring the questions raised by agnosticism and non-Christian believers.

How much attention do we pay in all this to the New Testament? It is in its name, of course, that the Christians who reject God have proclaimed the opposition between Jesus and God. Seeing Jesus as they do (especially the more politicized among them) as a free man and a liberator, and having an image of God that they judge to be also that of the Church, they had to postulate the rejection of God as a condition of access to Jesus. Their intuition is correct inasmuch as Jesus liberates us from an oppressive image of God. But acknowledging Jesus' freedom and admitting his liberating power still leaves his uniqueness out of account, so long as the freedom and power have not been situated in relation to the God that he invokes as his Father. To ignore Jesus' attitude to God is to be unfaithful to the New Testament. Certainly the New Testament does not provide us with the type of definition concerning the status of Jesus with regard to God as is laid down in the Councils of Nicaea (325) and Constantinople (381). But to disregard his attitude as a son, and the promise of the gift of the Spirit to believers is to distort the way in which Jesus presents himself as free and to pass over in silence that from which he frees us.

It is certainly true that Jesus frees us from God, but only inasmuch as God is our product. The metaphysical God who is the keystone of conservative ideology—so we are assured—is not the God witnessed to by the prophets and of whose kingdom Jesus preaches. In the present situation, many Christians who are oppressed by this image of God can perhaps express their faith in another God only by challenging the ancient God and his Church. But this seems to me a transitional phase. We shall have to return to the question of Jesus' God, of the God invoked as Father, who, far from destroying the freedom of Jesus' witness, reveals himself as its source, to such a degree that the New Testament declares that he freed Jesus from death.

We do not have to deny that Jesus was a free man and a liberator. What we have to do is *not* to make of Jesus the sum total of all our dreams and the only way of avoiding this temptation is by situating Jesus in his relation to God.

IV. CONCLUSION

From one point of view there is a positive element in the current movement of adherence to Jesus and rejection of God and the Church. It has highlighted the gaps in ecclesiastical teaching and practice, and it has drawn attention to the transposition that has been produced historically. It is our images of God that have defined Jesus and not Jesus who has destroyed our images of God. Moreover, it has denounced the retrogressive ideological function of the symbol of the divine fatherhood, and finally it has shown how much more sensitive the Church has always been to attacks on its organization and authority than to distortions of the gospel message.

Yet the movement does not escape a serious criticism. It has seen the relation between Jesus and God in the form of the dilemma: *either* Jesus *or* God. Thus it has fallen into the implicit thought-pattern of its adversaries, reinforcing by its rejection of God the dominant image, and despite the attention it pays to the historical uniqueness of Jesus, it makes of him a mythical figure through the privilege it accords him irrespective of all reference to God. This is doubtless a transitional failure and there are straws in the wind showing that thinking about God is regaining its true place among Christians. Our task will be to establish that the God of Jesus, far from wresting this man from his humanity, places him at the highest human point, for this God is God only where he brings freedom. So long as we think and practise Christianity under the sign of this either/or, whether we are contestatory or conservative, we shall not extricate ourselves from the oppositions which dominated inter-war theology (spiritual versus temporal, Church versus world, etc). It is not the absolutization of one of the poles of the dilemma that will free us from a mistaken way of thinking. The movements advocating adherence to Jesus have wanted to create an alternative way of living and thinking Christianity. They have, in my opinion, remained too much the prisoner of the thought-patterns of their adversaries to carry their objective through properly.

Translated by Barbara Wall

Josef Neuner

No Monopoly in promoting Freedom

IN VIEW of the biblical message of freedom, we must soberly examine in what sense the Christian claim of having brought liberty to mankind is justified. The biblical texts (Gal. 5. 5; 5. 13. Rom. 8. 2, etc.) seem to contain two assertions: (1) that Jesus Christ actually has brought freedom and that the Church in the fulfilment of Christ's mission is entrusted with the task of proclaiming liberation to mankind; (2) that the message of freedom in Jesus Christ is unique, which means that without him there would be no freedom. In the light of history, and particularly of modern secular culture, however, both assertions would seem to be best expressed as questions.

I. Two Questions

The early Church did in fact show itself to be a power of liberation. It had the strength to break through the socio-religious narrowness of its Judaic origin; above all, it had the courage to assert the freedom and personal responsibility of man before God in face of the totalitarian pretensions of the pagan state. The boldness to go even to death for the sake of this freedom turned out to be the victorious power of the youthful Church. This strength of the Church has been reawakened time and again in situations where the Church was forced into a struggle for freedom.

However, once the Church became the state religion, it had to integrate itself into the existing order. As partner of the existing system it often ceased to fulfil its prophetic role to stand up for the sovereignty of God and the freedom of men, and became a power of preservation of the existing order, even when this order was unjust. It would of course be unfair to make the Church responsible for all abuses, injustices and outrages of Western civilization, but one may legitimately ask whether it has fulfilled its prophetic role during the centuries when it was the undisputed spiritual power in Europe. When the French Revolution attacked the encrusted social structure in the name of freedom and equal human rights for all, the Church stood on the side of the ruling system. During the last century too a long time elapsed before, under Leo XIII, the Church took the part of the exploited workers against industrial oppression. Even today the Church seems in the eyes of most people, especially in developing countries, to be linked with the exploiting powers. It would certainly not be right to overlook the moderating and balancing influence of the Church in settling many conflicts. Still, one may sum up with Karl Rahner: "The Church cannot be silent about the historical guilt which it has accumulated in the course of centuries by defending the social conditions under which many groups of people had to suffer unjustly and gravely in very different societies and in very different ways."[1]

The claim of the Church to be the advocate of freedom was obscured even more by the lack of freedom within the Church. A Christian is aware of the Church's responsibility to proclaim the message of Jesus Christ without adulteration; he also agrees that the way of fulfilling this task had to be adjusted to varying historical situations. Still, there was too much intolerance and suppressed freedom of conscience in the battle against heresy. In defending Christian doctrine often the very essence of Christian life, true love, was denied, and the personal dignity and freedom of the other party disregarded.

Thus one may be justified in doubting whether the Church was always the champion of the freedom which is proclaimed in the Bible. On the other hand, throughout history we witness numerous advances towards freedom among the various nations. This

---

[1] K. Rahner, "Zur Theologie der Revolution", *Schriften zur Theologie* X, p. 585.

leads to the second question which concerns the uniqueness of the Christian message of freedom.

In the life of various nations, religion has proved not merely as a power of preserving and sanctioning the existing order, and hence of impeding spiritual and social freedom. It is also true that time and again it acted as a liberating force: in the vision of the seers which transcends the limitations of the empirical world, in the breakthrough of the divine love which does not allow itself to be fettered by religious systems and in prophetic challenges that share existing structures.

The Upanishadic literature of India tells us of such a breakthrough: there is the narration of Sanatkumāra who leads his disciples through the multitude of exterior experiences to the realization of the absolute, to fullness and bliss, and at the same time to the realization of the intimate Self, the *Ātman*, who dwells neither in the North nor in the South, neither above nor below, who is this whole world: "He who sees this, thinks this ... he is autonomous (*svarāj*), he has unlimited freedom in all worlds, whereas the others are "heteronomous (*anyarājan*), they have perishable worlds; in all worlds they have no freedom"[2]). Thus man finds freedom when liberated from the prison of senses and desires he realizes the true self.—Yājñavalkya, the greatest of the Upanishadic seers, leads to the same goal by another road. His disciple asks the supreme question: What remains of man when he dies, when whatever can be perceived of him returns to the elements: "when his breath goes into the wind, his eye into the sun ... his body into the earth ... what then becomes of this person?" Yājñavalkya withdraws the disciple from the assembly —because what follows is secret doctrine—and they speak about work (*karma*): "One becomes good by good action, bad by bad action"[3]). Man is more than the transient accumulation of elements, he is what he makes of himself, he is his freedom.

This search for liberation is common to all schools of Hinduism. One may agree with S. Radhakrishnan who finds the substance of India's religious tradition not in a set of doctrines, but in "a transforming experience", in its "power to transform

---

[2] *Chāngogya Upanishad*, 7.25.2.
[3] *Bṛhadāranyaka Upanishad*, 3.2.13.

man"[4]). This would have to be shown in a comprehensive survey of the philosophical systems, the schools of *bhakti*, which point out the way of personal love of God, of Tantrism, etc. But, however much they differ in their doctrine concerning the way of liberation, "all are agreed in regarding salvation as the attainment of the true status of the individual" (*ibid.*).

The same holds good, even more clearly, for Buddhism, which is based on the answer to the four questions: What is suffering, what is the cause of suffering, what is liberation from suffering, what is the way of liberation? Suffering in Buddhist understanding is not merely physical or mental pain, but consists in non-fulfilment, inadequacy. Freedom in Buddhism has a strongly ethical accent which even today puts it into contrast with Marxist materialism (notwithstanding apparent parallels), viz., that man is not determined by material conditions and social circumstances but determines his life himself.[5]—Similar observations can be made with regards to other religions. Thus we may legitimately conclude that at all times liberation and self-fulfilment belong to the aspirations of religious humanity as such, that freedom was searched for in many ways, that often it was found. Is it, then, possible to speak of an exclusively Christian message of freedom?

Today the Christian claim is challenged even more vigorously: Is not religion itself, even when it speaks of liberation, still a prison? The movement towards a non-religious secular humanism presents itself as the final exodus to human freedom. Our age has arrived at a new self-understanding of man which derives no longer from outside, but has man, and man alone, as the one valid starting-point. The Council also was aware of the new focus of man's self-realization: The Declaration on religious freedom does not begin with data from revelation but with the statement: "A sense of dignity of the human person has been impressing itself more and more deeply on the consciousness of contemporary man."[6] This new experience of man originates not from the Church but from man himself, it consists in his self-emanci-

---

[4] S. Radhakrishnan, *Eastern Religion and Western Thought* ([2]1940), p. 21.

[5] Cf. Ernst Benz, *Buddhas Wiederkehr* (1963), pp. 255–74.

[6] Declaration, *Dignitatis Humanae*, on Religious Freedom, 1.

pation, in the turn from a theocentric to an anthropocentric understanding of the world.

The Middle Ages considered cosmos and history as the unfolding of a divine plan of creation and salvation. All order in the world was based on divine law, the social, political and above all the ecclesiastical structures were sanctioned by divine authority and man's knowledge came primarily from divine revelation and was interpreted by the Church. Thus man could not really speak and decide for himself. He had no right to inquire on his own into nature and its laws. The scientific experiment was suspected to be presumptuous on man's part and a challenge to the word of God. The riddles of man and universe remained unexplored.[7]

Today man makes himself the centre of the world and the lord of his own history. Nature and cosmos are no longer the pre-established immutable frames into which he has to fit himself, but the material of which he builds his future. No longer does he accept his future from a providence that eludes his calculations but he expects it from science and technology in which he has discovered the instruments to transform the world and to manipulate his future. Discriminating social and legal regulations, the unequal distribution of goods, are no longer structures that are not to be touched, they are challenged as usurped power positions against which he protests in the name of basic human rights. Modern man is no longer satisfied with the material uplift of his living conditions but seeks the complete liberation which opens the way to a fulfilled human existence.[8]

This awakening to freedom is witnessed in all spheres of human life. In the realm of politics we are contemporaries of the establishment of democratic governments and the process of decolonization; the demand for the social liberation of all is loud and urgent, particularly in developing countries. Women gain more and more equality with men. Youth refuses to live under tutelage and demands co-responsibility in shaping its own life and training. We encounter the increasing protest against a sexual morality which "reflects to a great extent the fear of women and the deep-rooted religious suspicion of sex", and the desire for "a

[7] Cf. H. R. Schlette, *Christen als Humanisten* (1967), pp. 23–8.
[8] Cf. K. Rahner, *op. cit.*

more positive theology of sexuality which is grateful for freedom, joy and creative power".[9] Human freedom lays hold on the future and is determined to plan the "hominization of man's surroundings; out of a world which formerly he took for granted, man has made the quarry for the construction of such a world which he will be ready to acknowledge as his own".[10]

So we live in the midst of a symphony of freedom played with all the instruments of the modern world. Is it still possible to hear in it the freedom message of the gospel?

II. CHRISTIAN CRITIQUE OF THE MESSAGES OF FREEDOM

What has the Christian to say about these messages of freedom, religious and secular? He surely has to acknowledge the common aspiration of all ages to find freedom. Man wants to be truly himself in unbroken existence, freed from narrowing, splitting, repressing powers. Though there is a great variety in the concrete answers to the quest for freedom, one may say, with some simplification, that man seeks his freedom in four dimensions: in his origin, in his final expectation, in his interiority, and finally also in selfish isolation.

At all times man felt himself linked to his origin, to the dawn of his existence when his life and his world originated in unimpaired fullness and vigour. M. Eliade assures us that "it would be impossible to overstress the tendency observable in every society, however highly developed, to bring back that time, the mythical time, the Great Time".[11] This is the case most of all among agrarian cultures where life is woven into the cycle of the seasons, and the origin of all life is celebrated on the solstice, or on the feasts of sowing and harvesting. These feasts are not recreation but duty, because the renewal of fertility depends on their celebration. The wild orgies which often mark these feasts do not mean the breakdown of moral order but are the performance of a necessary ritual. According to Eliade the "excesses fulfil

[9] Gr. Baumann, "Tendenzen der Katholischen Sexualmoral", *Orientierung*, Dec. 1972, p. 272.

[10] K. Rahner, "Heilsauftrag der Kirche und Humanisierung der Welt", *Schriften zur Theologie* X, p. 554.

[11] M. Eliade, *Patterns of Comparative Religion* (1958), p. 395.

a definite and useful role in the economy of the sacred. They break down the barrier between man, society, nature and gods. ... What was emptied of substance is replenished, what was shattered into fragments becomes one again, what was in isolation merges into the great womb of all things. The orgies set flowing the sacred energy of life."[12] The return to the formless, chaotic origin, to the condition of freedom and fullness offers the renewed assurance of energy and fertility.

The other dimension in which man seeks freedom and fulfilment is the future. At all times men have hoped for the return of the golden age and the final liberation from the prison of physical want and social fetters. It is significant that Marxism, the most energetic movement of our age, again proclaims a secular messianism of liberation.

Most significant for our time is the shifting of freedom into man's interiority. In the West it has been known primarily through the Stoa: man finds happiness independently of exterior conditions as health, money, honour. Freedom is found in man himself; what takes place outside himself is not decisive. He lives his true life within himself, in undisturbed detachment from the world (*apatheia*).

This transfer of the realm of freedom into man's interiority is characteristic of the Eastern religions which are distinguished by their withdrawal from the world. J. A. Cuttat describes the spiritual attitude of the East: "Becoming is a centrifugal movement from reality to unreality." Creation means diminution, loss of fullness. "Correspondingly all Eastern ways leading to the Divine ... consist of an inner counteract which neutralizes this centrifugal evolution by a symmetrically inverse involution. ... This implies a radical detachment from the world as such, not only from evil, as peripheric illusion, including the empirical ego."[13] Man becomes free by withdrawing from the world. Patanjali defines Yoga as "elimination of empirical modifications of consciousness" (*cittavṛtti nirodaḥ*). It follows that the world of becoming, the unfolding of history, is excluded from the realm of man's freedom. The real world moves on in unending neces-

[12] M. Eliade, *op. cit.*, p. 356.
[13] J. A. Cuttat, *The Spiritual Dialogue between East and West* (1961), p. 18.

sary cycles, it is not saved. Rather it is man—his spiritual principle—that is liberated from the world.

These are admittedly simplified formulas. One will readily recognize that modern Hinduism takes pain to come to a new, more positive understanding of world and progress (though one may ask how far this takes place under the influence of Christianity). But such reflections are outside our theme. We are engaged in the inquiry of how the Christian idea of freedom can become the critique and inspiration for the messages of freedom in our world.

Christian freedom is liberation of the whole man. It comprises all that is contained in the above-mentioned systems. It is freedom in his origin, in the creative power of the Spirit. It is freedom in fulfilment in the eschatological promise towards which we are moving. It is also gift of the present saeculum, lived and suffered not in secluded interiority but in the harsh reality of our sinful race, often helpless, "given up to death for Jesus' sake so that the life of Jesus may be manifested in our mortal flesh" (2 Cor. 4. 11). Thus Christian freedom permeates the whole being of man and does not allow an escape, no flight into the origin nor into the future, nor into the inner realm. It is participation in the freedom of Jesus Christ who has assumed and liberated the whole of our human existence.

Hence the Christian critique of all freedom messages consists in searching questions. Does, for example, the proclaimed and promised freedom truly mean the whole man, man with his world, present and to come, or only one section of it? Is it a withdrawal into the mythos of origin, or a vague escape into the coming world to console us over the present distress? Or is it an emigration from the reality of the world and the responsibility of service into an inner sphere? Any such "freedom" would be unmasked as illusion and condemned by Christ, the true Saviour.

The Christian critique goes still further. Christian freedom means life through the Spirit and building the new community of men in him. It cannot lead to the isolation of the individual ego and its narrow interests. Already Paul knew this easiest and most frequent perversion of the freedom message when it is misused as the cheap façade for selfishness and uncharitableness:

"For me there are no forbidden things" (1 Cor. 6. 12). Freedom which is moved no longer by the unifying and life-giving Spirit, which no longer builds up Christ's body, becomes subservient to the powers of disintegration. Paul does not acknowledge a freedom that stands in itself: unless freedom is in the service of Christ, it becomes slavery of sin. This is the fourth dimension in which man can evade the challenge of genuine freedom. The Christian critique, therefore, has to ask serious questions about the many forms of freedom which are being proclaimed today. True, secularization means liberation, but it must be warned that we are drawn into "a movement which may lead either to greater freedom or to new enslavement. . . . To imagine that secularity can, so to speak, stand alone, would be to fall into an ideology which would end by enslaving man."[14] Freedom and responsibility must remain together.

Therefore a Christian will also be cautious when freedom and revolution are mentioned in one breath. If revolution is the transition to another system of power it only means an exchange of roles in the old game of lord and slave. Freedom is where the new man is born who "is created in God's way, in the goodness and holiness of the truth" (Eph. 4. 24).

III. Service in the Liberation of the World

If we propose the liberation in Christ as the norm and critique of any other freedom, as we have done just now, are we then not setting up again a Christian monopoly of liberation?

This is not the case. In fact, unless we presuppose something in common between the Christian and other conceptions of freedom it would not even be possible to judge the freedom movements of religions and of our time from the point of view of Christ.—In the following at least an indication of the christological understanding of this common ground is outlined. The theological foundations of these reflections must be presupposed.

When speaking about the relation of Christian freedom to freedom in the world, religious and secular, we actually deal only with one particular application of the much wider problem of the

[14] L. Newbigin, *Honest Religion for Secular Man* (1966), p. 136.

relation of Jesus Christ to the created world. We cannot isolate Jesus Christ and take him out of the context of the religious and profane history of mankind. We cannot speak of him as the only light in the sense that everything else is darkness. This is no longer possible in view of the ever-widening richness of insights gained from the history of religions, of the secular values of our age, and most of all of the deeper theological perspectives which have found expression in the Council. The uniqueness of Jesus Christ must be understood as inclusive, not exclusive. This may be spelled out in brief.

There is only one God who is Creator, Lord of all things, and Father of Our Lord Jesus Christ. All history from the hidden origins of created beings to the expected fulfilment in the heavenly city derives from the one divine design of creation and salvation. This design, "the *mysterion* which through the ages was hidden in God, who created all things" (Eph. 3. 9) has been finally and without ambiguity revealed and irrevocably realized in Jesus Christ. All nations are included in one and the same mystery of sin and grace, servitude and liberation, or, more correctly, this very mystery of slavery and liberation unfolds in the history of mankind, not only in religious systems but in every movement by which our race grows towards its fuller self-understanding and self-realization. This unfolding in the history of mankind is not a casual game in which various possibilities are played at random side by side, but God has shown once and for all in Jesus Christ what man is and what human freedom means. In him the true meaning of freedom is shown for all men.

Thus Jesus Christ is the norm for all that is human: "the words of Christ are at one and the same time words of judgment and grace, of death and life".[15] Does such a normative claim not imply the narrowing of the scope of man? This would be the case if one were to absolutize the historico-cultural situation of the earthly Jesus in Palestine. But this would be the reversal of the Christian message of freedom. Jesus Christ means the acknowledgment, liberation, fulfilment of all that is human. This is the meaning attributed by the Council to the finality of the

---

[15] Decree, *Ad Gentes*, on the Church's Missionary Activity, 8.

revelation in Jesus Christ: it is not a limitation, but the all comprising promise of salvation, "that God is with us to free us from the darkness of sin and death and to raise us up to life eternal".[16] Christ does not represent one section or one phase of human history that could be overtaken by further developments, but the total call to, and promise of, freedom for our entire race. The struggle for this freedom pervades the length and breadth of our history.

Thus a Christian is not astonished or bewildered that wherever God is at work, there is also the message of freedom. He will not suspect such messages as rivalry. At the same time he ought to develop a fine sense of discernment and ask whether these messages are genuine, whether they diminish or disfigure the true freedom, whether they are not a masked escape from the hard realities of life, a refusal of service, a retirement to oases of illusionary freedom by which man would absent himself from the drama of actual history. He is able to judge these ideas of freedom through the word of God and the inner testimony of the Spirit that makes him experience the freedom which is in Christ Jesus.

The Church must have at heart the service for the freedom of all men. In the Church itself there must be responsible freedom which allows each one to fulfil his Christian vocation—this is, according to Vatican II, the meaning of the ecclesiastical office.[17] In the modern world it must be prophet and champion of the freedom for all men. It also must protect the responsibility of freedom against degeneration lest it be used as trademark for the selling out of man's dignity.

[16] *Dei Verbum* 4. As to the wider context, cf. Vorgrimler, *Commentary on the Documents of Vatican II*, vol. III, pp. 176 f.
[17] Constitution, *Lumen Gentium*, on the Church, 18.

Dieter Lührmann

Jesus: History and Remembrance

IN the history of mankind the name of Jesus has implied both freedom and unfreedom. It would be near-dissimulation for Christians to deny that. They would run the risk of the same accusation if they ignored the fact that the modern Western understanding of freedom as the individual right to unrestricted self-realization was prompted to a considerable degree by traditions other than Christianity. German Protestant theology in particular has always been very suspicious of these traditions forged in the French Revolution of 1789.

It would be dishonest to try to legitimate this modern notion of freedom in an *interpretatio christiana* in Jesus, and then to elevate it to a concept of freedom which was "effective" only in this interpretation. On the other hand, reference to Jesus can help to disclose other elements which were just as meaningful in the development of Western tradition. Perhaps they will evoke new thinking in this regard, which is needed in view of the obvious crisis in the Western notion of freedom, which is grounded in the liberty of the individual.

The question is all the more severe for the German Protestant tradition inasmuch as *the* christological problem of modern times (the quest for the historical Jesus), as it has been posed, is closely involved with the fate of liberalism in Germany—and, more precisely, that of the cosmopolitan brand of liberalism which tried to latch onto West European traditions.

In his *Geschichte der Leben-Jesu-Forschung* (sixth edition 1961, ch. 14), Albert Schweitzer also censured this liberal version of Jesus. The historical Jesus posited by the liberals was made in the image of a nineteenth-century liberal, not of the Jesus who lived in Palestine between A.D. 1 and 30.

Instead Schweitzer saw Jesus as the stranger, the unknown and nameless, who not only preached but lived a scandalously alien eschatology, but who has in certain aspects remained an inspiration up to the present day.

A somewhat different picture is obtained from the lectures on the "Essence of Christianity" with which Adolf Harnack began the new year in the winter semester of 1899–1900. Schweitzer's judgment is not so plausible today: "In his *Essence of Christianity* Harnack almost entirely obscures the way in which Jesus' teaching is conditioned by chronological history and addresses himself only to a Gospel which he finds no difficulty in fitting to the year 1899." Yet Harnack's account of Christianity was one of the most illustrious of its times; he paid attention to such problems as culture, labour and law, in a presentation of Jesus' proclamation which did indeed include the "essence of Christianity".

Harnack's book is a classic document of the liberal quest for the historical Jesus, which reveals typical strengths and weaknesses of that approach. Even though he is careful to avoid a biography of Jesus since the texts cannot offer enough evidence of the development of Jesus' personality (of the kind essential for a biography in the nineteenth-century mode), according to Harnack what we know is enough for a "character-study" of Jesus. Jesus himself had understood himself as the son of God, and if his proclamation is correctly understood it also offers yardsticks for the year 1899 and the imminent twentieth century.

Hence, in the quest for the "essence of Christianity", dogmatics is dissolved by history, the confessional Christ by the historical Jesus, and the persona of traditional christology by the "personality" of Jesus (cf. R. Slenczka, *Geschichtlichkeit und Personsein Jesu Christi,* 1967). Neither then nor at any time in subsequent decades was the problem of the historical Jesus in any way an arbitrary question, but instead the central problem of the basis and content of Christianity. Of course for Harnack and his time it seemed to be decided in favour of historical criticism, which succeeded in offering a specific systematic picture of Christianity.

The animosity of the confrontation and the harshness of the theses in the dispute are perhaps hardly comprehensible outside the German Protestant tradition. It is part of the special context of this confrontation that the struggle was directed not only against traditional dogmatics, which mainly in the course of the nineteenth century had been compelled to abandon an increasing number of its positions. The secret opponent was much more Hegel's theological philosophy. Its application in the works of David Friedrich Strauss and Bruno Bauer to the historical Jesus as the ground and cause of Christianity was the actual stimulus which brought theology to join historicism as the only way to resist Hegel and his disciples. To this area we owe the formation of the two-source theory, a theory in which it was hoped it would be possible to get closer to the historical Jesus in contradistinction to the speculative Christ of the Hegelians. Here, too, belongs the understanding of which criteria to apply in order to distinguish the historically "true" from the false or "speculative".

With the personality and proclamation of the historical Jesus as the historically assured sum total of Christianity we are brought back to Harnack. And Harnack himself had to take account of the blows which threatened to undermine this basis. For example, the rediscovery of early-Christian eschatology. In the course of the nineteenth century an increasing number of apocalypses that had been forgotten in the tradition of the Western Church were made accessible (cf. the editions by Kautzsch and Charles at the turn of the century). Johannes Weiss and Albert Schweitzer recognized their significance for an understanding of primitive Christianity as the historical Jesus. The kingdom of God now became a transcendent magnitude (Weiss), and the way of Jesus was comprehensible only as an immeasurable hope in an apocalyptic metamorphosis (Schweitzer). Both were disposed of by the non-occurrence of the Parousia —but what vanished before anything else was the liberal theological concept of the kingdom of God.

Harnack was still able to accommodate it by speaking of two crucial points on an "elliptical notion" of the kingdom of God.

But he could not understand the frontal attack that dialectical theology mounted on liberal theology. This is shown in his public correspondence with Karl Barth. The diastasis between the historical Jesus, who is irrelevant for Christianity, and the kerygmatic Christ, who determines the norm and essence of Christianity, is wholly comprehensible only in the context of this opposition to liberal theology. The plan of Bultmann's *Jesus* (1926) shows a remarkable reliance on Harnack's *Essence of Christianity* that is not at all fortuitous.

This Jesus book does not, of course, betray anything of the aforementioned diastasis itself. At the time it *could* also be taken in the sense of the old problematics as a presentation of the sum of Christianity—though of a Christianity that now, by reason of the emphasis placed on eschatology, appeared somewhat withdrawn from the world. Of course it was at a very early date in Bultmann's œuvre that the "kerygma" assumed the role of basis and cause of Christianity that had been played by the historical Jesus in liberal theology.

In this situation even Martin Kähler's essay "Der sogenante historische Jesus und der historische, biblische Christus" (The so-called historical Jesus and the historical, biblical Christ) received attention for the claim that the real Jesus is not the historical but the proclaimed Jesus. This thesis finds support in the development of form-history as the appropriate historical approach to the New Testament texts. If the literary criticism of the nineteenth century sought for reliable sources for the historical Jesus, form-history saw that the New Testament texts were primarily and above all sources for the history of the community and its particular confession. That meant a methodological displacement of the supposed right way to the historical Jesus. The gospel texts were to be scrutinized for the community which handed them down, and the kerygma basic to it.

What does "kerygma" mean in this connection? (cf. H. Ott's article "Kerygma" in RGG[3], Vol. 3, pp. 1250–4). It cannot be established from certain NT texts such as 1 Cor. 15. 3b–5, however much this text is, like others, kerygma. Kerygma is the proclamation of the salvific meaning of Jesus—of the crucified and risen Jesus, who—as the present proclamation—offers salvation to the faithful. That leads, in Bultmann, to an existential interpretation as the only one that (in his opinion) is appropriate —as an interpretation of the mythological statements of the New Testament already offered in the New Testament itself.

In 1959 Bultmann himself had discerned the difference between the historical Jesus and the kerygma in the following three points (R. Bultmann, *Exegetica,* 1967, pp. 446 ff):

"1. The historical person of Jesus (in so far as it is visible to the critical eye in the synoptic gospels) is replaced in the kerygma by the mythic figure of the son of God.

"2. Whereas the preaching of Jesus is the eschatological and indeed apparent kingdom of God, in the kerygma Jesus Christ is proclaimed as the One who died on the cross as a representative for the sins of men and was miraculously raised up by God for our salvation. In the theological thinking of Paul and John, the decisive eschatological event has thus already happened.

"3. In the case of Jesus the eschatological proclamation is closely accompanied by the proclamation of the will of God— the call to radical obedience under the divine ordinances which culminate in the commandment of love. Of course the kerygma does not omit ethical preaching. But when Paul and John connect ethical requirements and above all the commandment of Love with the kerygma of Christ, they do not do so by repeating Jesus' interpretation of the will of God from the Synoptics. In the confessional formulations of the kerygma (the first Christian creeds) this is not taken up at all, and in the typical early-Christian doctrinal and admonitory writings, the ethical parenesis takes second place."

It should not be overlooked in this context that Bultmann has always emphasized that the kerygma itself is an historical given, and one including an historical datum—the cross of Jesus.

At this point there began the new quest for the historical Jesus: if the kerygma was in fact an historical given of this kind, and its substance was Jesus of Nazareth, an historical individual, surely one then must ask what support that kerygma had in that individual and his activity. Consistently, Bultmann refused this approach, denounced it as an historical safeguard for faith, and always suspected it of being a mere return to the life-of-Jesus theology of the liberals.

Let us pause a moment at this point. The antithesis of the

historical Jesus and the kerygmatic Christ is, according to the foregoing, the consequence of a new consideration of the ground and cause of Christianity, which was reluctant henceforth to allow its content to be predicated on the basis of the actual situation, but—however strange this might seem—wished to work from the New Testament texts. The connection between those texts and the present day was not to be found in impulses which emanated from Jesus and might still be effective in some way, but in the kerygma as it directly related to man, now as then, and concerned him in his actual situation. That the withdrawal from liberalism does not (as the liberals feared) mean a disappearance of the world-relatedness of faith was something that Bultmann himself constantly stated, not least emphatically at the end of his comparison of the ancient and the Christian understanding of freedom (*Glauben und Verstehen*, vol. 4, 1965, pp. 42–51). Hence the individualism for which Bultmann is reproached is always open to the social responsibility of the individual; on the other hand, the outward determination of the individual is subsumed theologically under the concept of the law and sin.

But we must return to the "new quest for" the historical Jesus. In his famous essay opening the discussion, Ernst Käsemann deduced the legitimacy of a revived quest for the historical Jesus from the fact that the evangelists themselves tend to "historicize" as well as to "kerygmatize" their narratives. For the evangelists the content of the gospel depends on what the historical, or truly "earthly", Jesus said and did.

What Käsemann posited here of the final stage of tradition, the evangelists, does not of course apply exclusively to them. However true it may be that the gospels and the vehicles of the tradition previous to them narrate not out of historical interest in the historical individual Jesus, but in order to proclaim the Lord present in his community, nevertheless the transference of the kerygma notion, mainly derived from Pauline and Johannine materials, to the history of the synoptic tradition, appears one-sided. On the way between Jesus (as the starting-point of tradition) and the evangelists there is a tradition which discerns the salvation that has come with Jesus (the Lord present here too) in his words and deeds, and sees its own proclamation as a continuation of the salvific proclamation of Jesus.

That has taken very different forms. I would allude only to the equipping of the disciples with the pneumatic power that Jesus gave them after the speeches of commission, and whose efficacy is reported in the Acts of the Apostles. Here Jesus is the first who really has control over the powers of illness and death, and at the same time he is the present Lord who enables his community to continue his activity. A similar concept is at the basis of certain groups which received the proclamation of Jesus, for instance the so-called "logia-source" (Q). Here Jesus' death is interpreted in the perspective of the testimony of the violent fate of the prophets, and his resurrection as establishment as the son of God (Lk. 10. 22 par.), who alone mediates the salvation promised by the Father. But salvation is understood here as a pronouncement of the law and as a promise of deliverance from that judgment for those who belong to Jesus the son of man. The ultimate consequence (admittedly with an abandonment of eschatology) is drawn in the first words of the gospel of Thomas: "Whoever discovers the meaning of these words will not taste death."

Hence there are groups in the New Testament whose communities look upon themselves as in continuity with the earthly Jesus. Therefore not all consider the (according to Paul, appropriate) difference between the earthly and the risen Jesus to be legitimate. Here discontinuity in Paul is countered by a theology which lives from continuity. Therefore we cannot consider the development of the Jesus-traditions from the sole viewpoint of the kerygma, but have to inquire into its own laws. That poses once again the question of the historical Jesus. The handing on of the words and deeds of Jesus was in no way an insignificant matter in these groups, but followed from a particular christological and soteriological interest. That also has consequences in regard to the methodological question of the determination of the original Jesus material. For we now have to take into account the fact that the community had Jesus' words and deeds as the yardstick for their own words and deeds. Of course they could form Jesus' words anew by recourse to the ever-present Lord, yet those words had to be measured by Jesus' own.

Perhaps the category of "anamnesis" (remembrance) will be of some use in this new approach to the Jesus traditions in the New Testament (cf. O. Michel, article on *mimneskomai* in *Theologisches Wörterbuch z. NT*, vol. 4, pp. 678–87; N. A. Dahl, "*Anamnesis*", Studia Theologica 1 (1948), pp. 69–95). Bultmann treated "anamnesis" in contradistinction to "existence" only as "*mere* remembrance"—historical reminiscence without significance for the present behaviour of Christians. Julius Schniewind, on the other hand, pointed out that "for the New Testament, anamnesis and the Christ event belong wholly together" (*Kerygma und Mythos*, vol. 1, ed. H. W. Bartsch, 1951², p. 104). He cites a number of passages, but takes his evaluation somewhat beyond Schniewind's rather too thetic proposition: "confidence in the reliability of the matter handed down, in the reliability of the message, is essentially *fiducia*, and accords with the fiducial faith of *pro me*."

"Anamnesis" is not only recalling an event which then guarantees the reliability of the report of that event—often eyewitnesses are the worst of all witnesses, for they have not understood the event in the least. Anamnesis has a second and more important perspective as far as the New Testament is concerned: in the texts cited by Schniewind the particular community is reminded of that which is the basis and cause of their Christian existence. That which is remembered is the standard upon which a present decision is grounded. Even the description of the gospels found in Justin as "memories of the apostles" is not meant univocally in the nineteenth-century sense as "memoirs of the apostles", but as a presentation of what the apostles recall as the foundation of Christianity.

If we examine the use of "remember" in early Christian literature, it is not surprising that the variegated mass of diverse norms is reflected in the particular objects of remembering, but all are one in asserting that christology as such is the norm, whereas they take different views of the content of christology. With "do you not know", Paul reminds his communities of the kerygma of the salvific meaning of the death and resurrection of Jesus. In the gospel of John the post-paschal anamnesis discloses the meaning of the pre-paschal events, which without the Easter experiences would remain devoid of sense. Especially in the anti-heretical disputes of early Christianity that "remembrance" of the basis becomes a fixed *topos*.

In the handing-down of the word of Jesus, which even in the second century still occurred to a considerable extent independently of the already existing gospels (later adopted into the canon), there is a "recalling" of the words of Jesus as a fixed introductory formula for quotations. In the New Testament there is an indication of this in Acts 20. 35. In fact the origin of the gospels is incomprehensible without such a remembrance of the pre-Easter Jesus. The evangelist Matthew enjoins upon his community what Jesus has commanded (Mt. 28. 19) and refers back to the great complex of addresses in the gospel, especially the Sermon on the Mount. Only doing the word of Jesus, which is identical with doing the will of the Father, opens the way to salvation, the kingdom of heaven.

A christology of this kind is already available in the tradition-history of the material collected by Matthew into the Sermon on the Mount: one's relation to Jesus' words represents one's relation to salvation. That means, on the other hand, that the words of Jesus were handed down for the sake of that very relationship. Remembrance of the earthly Jesus is in this case remembrance of the disclosure of salvation.

Hence the New Testament co-features under the aspect of *anamnesis* or remembrance quite diverse conceptions of memoirs. They first come together in the second century, and then not without weighty disputes; and the tension between them is one of the essential motives of the formation of dogma in the early Church, and of later ecclesiastical tradition right down to our own days. In the course of the Church's history there have always been groups which have protested against the contemporary Church in the name of Jesus.

Of course it would be wrong to think that with this new consideration of the character of the gospel tradition the theological problem of the historical Jesus is already resolved. Initially it can be determined only that there were groups in the early Church who saw the pre-paschal Jesus as the beginning and foundation of Christianity. It was a mistake of liberal theology to identify these groups with the historical Jesus himself. Form-history has shown that *report* is not identical with *that which is reported*—but that is true of all history, and not only of the special problem of the historical Jesus. What form-history of course neglected was the multitude of phenomena which it subsumed under the single notion of kerygma.

The quest for the historical Jesus also becomes more pressing as a methodological problem, if the thesis outlined hitherto is accepted. A layer of primitive-Christian tradition which expressly handed down Jesus' words and deeds for the sake of salvation *has to be* examined to decide how its tradition relates to its starting-point, the words and deeds *of Jesus*. Only in this way is it possible to decide what "Easter" meant for these groups, and whence they derived the legitimation for their assertion of continuity with Jesus. On the other hand, another question is also pressing: that of the support such a theology finds in Jesus himself. Is there a road from the circle which Jesus summoned as his disciples to the community of Jesus which confesses him?

From this initially historical problem the theological problem arises anew—a question that cannot be resolved simply by recourse to liberal theology. Christology cannot be reduced to an historically demonstrable Jesus. Precisely those early Christian groups who hand down their tradition out of a *soteriological* interest speak against that. Soteriology does not reside in (however heavily obligatory) impulses emanating from the historical Jesus. And ecclesiology is not a mere imitative theology. Throughout the history of the Church it has been shown, however, that Jesus' words were criticism of the Church and could remove from the contemporary Church that legitimation it derived from the same Jesus, in order to open up a new future for the Church as well as for individual Christians.

What are the implications of these points for the theme of "freedom"? Paul and John, each in his own way, recalling their determination of the basis of Christianity, called "freedom" the consequence of salvation disclosed in Jesus. Of course it is a freedom from the law, from sin, from death (Paul), a freedom from the world (John), and therefore freedom not as a realization of human autonomy but as a liberation of man, not least of all from himself.

In the synoptic Jesus tradition the theme of "freedom" is never referred to, and we may therefore presume, with all the usual reservations, to say that Jesus himself never adverted to this theme. But "freedom" certainly does occur in modern interpretations of the discourse and activity of Jesus: as freedom from inherited bonds (Jesus' attitude to the law), as freedom from social and religious barriers (Jesus' attitude to tax-gatherers and prostitutes), and as freedom of man for his neighbour (the commandment of love). Ernst Käsemann asked: "Was Jesus liberal?", and answered his question with a play on the Chalcedonian formulas: "pious and liberal at the same time" (*Der Ruf der Freiheit*, 1968, pp 28–58).

Käsemann's statement shows that even Jesus' freedom can only be talked about as all christological statements have always been formulated: as *polemical* statements. Wherever *unfreedom* is practised in the name of Jesus, the name of Jesus must be invoked for the cause of freedom.

Of course Jesus, his words and his actions will always escape any attempt simply to misuse them to legitimate theologies which are grounded in themselves and obtain their contents from other sources. Over the Christian community, which experienced the stormy years of bellicose disputes between Jews and Romans up to the Jewish War, there was Jesus' unremitting commandment to love their enemies; and they could not explain that commandment away as obviously out of date, in the way in which the Maccabees once interpreted the commandment about the sabbath in view of military requirements.

The above-mentioned interpretations of Jesus by recourse to the category of "freedom" are banal so long as they do not define that notion more exactly in the perspective of Jesus' proclamation of the kingdom of God and his justice. Freedom is first and foremost the freedom *of God*, and as Jesus referred to it freedom is liberation, not an allusion to a naturally human right.

The recalling of Jesus' freedom in contradistinction to the inherited interpretation of the law as shown in the gospels in Jesus' disputes with Pharisees and exegetes, is also—in the community which hands down these disputes—not merely confirmation of what that community itself practises but a enjoining of the community to obey the commandment of love as a consequence of the freedom donated by God. And the recalling of

Jesus' attitude to tax-collectors and prostitutes was certainly not, for later Christian generations, an approach to be made practicable only by reservations. Every community acknowledging Jesus is faced with the dilemma that it is able to live out a fundamental openness to others, whether they are tax-collectors, prostitutes or anyone, only at the price of their own organization.

Freedom, therefore, is not a right to which everyone can lay claim, but that freedom which is given by God and which puts in question the right of the individual because it is always and primarily the freedom of the other as well. And that is the mystery of the justice of the kingdom of God: that it seems to invert the rights of man. The beatitudes at the beginning of the Sermon on the Mount show that very clearly, if they are read not as exhortation for whoever *feels,* poor, sad, and so on, but to whoever *is* so. One does not acquire a claim to the kingdom of God by entering into the role of a poor man or a mourner; instead the kingdom of God is promised to those who hold that to be impossible.

The crisis of the modern understanding of freedom has one of its causes in the fact that reality has dismissed the optimistic expectation that the problems of society would be instantly solved if only human rights were constitutionally guaranteed. The freedoms guaranteed thus emerge as freedoms which not everyone can acquire, and as individual freedoms they fail to take in vast areas of life.

Theology and the Church have no cause to rejoice at the failure of this liberal ideology in the guise of those who always knew that it wouldn't work out so nicely. Theology and the Church never stood outside the general movements of their time, whether they reacted positively or negatively to them. To that extent, they too participate in this crisis of the understanding of freedom. Precisely if they are enjoined by their foundation in Jesus to look for the rights *of others,* they must help to direct men's eyes to where elementary human rights are abused, and cannot close their own eyes while calling in excuse upon the crisis in the understanding of freedom.

Freedom from the world is far too often proclaimed negatively in the name of Jesus as distance from the world, which is assessed as evil. But Jesus himself referred his audience to their experiences with the world in a very basic way. In the parables he uses the circumstances of this world to make clear how it is with the kingdom of heaven. Admittedly nature itself is not revelation; it does not show directly who God is. It is the *creation* of God. But what does a reference to the birds of the air and the lilies of the field (Mt. 6. 25 ff par.) mean in view of the modern apocalyptic threat of a "dumb spring" in which no birds will sing and no flowers bloom?? Here too a theology that invokes Jesus cannot look on happily and just find more evidence for its analysis of the world. The world must be seen not as one's own divinized given, and not as a demonized evil power—but as God's creation which must not (made over in a new way by men) turn against men.

Such reflections on the category of freedom can point to the consequences of a new quest for the historical Jesus. To a large extent, in a confrontation with the Johannine or Pauline understanding of freedom, they would not lead to essentially different results. Their special nature is that the claim of the proclamation of Jesus is not only an ethically motivating call to action, but calls in question man himself in the perspective of the kingdom of God, in so far as he takes his stand on his own right; it also refers him to the rights of others. The freedom which Jesus disclosed is not that which is obviously proper to every man, but that which is unexpected—and to a great degree also incomprehensible.

Remembering Jesus therefore does not mean reminding man of what he already knows, but reminding him that the kingdom of God and his justice precede man and summon him to consider the rights of others. This delineates the area in which Christian theology is allowed to love, and demarcation lines are clearly marked which it is forbidden to cross. To that extent Jesus' proclamation does contain norms which define what Christianity can be in its time. The dispute will continue about the realization of those norms, and a criterion will be available in the fact that Christian theology will never be self-sufficient. In all times, in the people of God of the Old and New Covenant, prophet has stood against prophet, and a criterion for true prophecy has seldom been a modernity, but rather an invocation of old, buried or disavowed traditions.

Perhaps that kind of prophecy in the discussion of freedom will once again serve to express the old and obscured theme of God's kingdom and his justice, and will then probably also— as was always the fate of prophecy in the past—have to turn it against the Church itself. Yet to be rejected was the destiny of prophets even before those who in the name of Jesus turned the experience of atrocity into the stuff of ultimate glory.

Translated by Verdant Green

Rudolf Pesch

Jesus, a Free Man

ONE of the encouraging features of recent theology is its increasing success in describing the way in which Jesus of Nazareth
was "true man", a man like the other men of his time and "the
true man". Jesus is presented as a charismatic figure with
prophetic features or as a prophet with charismatic powers.[1] It
is no longer taboo to talk about Jesus' faith, and he can be regarded as the authentic believer who founded the new faith.[2]
Jesus' claim can be described as the claim of the last messenger
calling Israel to be the people of God of the eschatological era.[3]
Jesus' messianic consciousness, his personal consciousness and
the communication between him and his disciples can also,
after a period which restricted the approach to such questions
in the name of historical rigour, be given a new treatment.[4]
The fact that, in current discussion, the freedom of Jesus should
arouse new interest is not surprising, though in view of the

[1] Cf. M. Hengel, *Nachfolge und Charisma* (BZNW 34), Berlin, 1968;
R. Pesch, "Zur theologischen Bedeutung der Machttaten Jesu. Reflexionen
eines Exegeten", *Theol. Quartalschrift* 152 (1972), pp. 203–13.
[2] Cf. D. O. Via, *Die Gleichnisse Jesu* (Munich, 1970); K. Rahner and
W. Thüsing, *Christologie—systematisch und exegetisch* (Freiburg, 1972);
R. Pesch, "Der Glaube Jesu", *Christ in der Gegenwart* 24 (1972), pp.
221 ff.
[3] Cf. R. Pesch, "Der Anspruch Jesu", *Orientierung* 35 (1971), pp. 53–
56, 67–70, 77–81; "Thesen zur Sache Jesu", *Herder-Korrespondenz* 26
(1971), pp. 33 ff.
[4] Cf. R. Pesch, "Das Messias-Bekenntnis des Petrus (Mk. 8. 27–30).
Neuverhandlung einer alten Frage", *Bibl. Zeitschrift* (Neue Folge) 17
(1973), 18 (1974).

long history of Jesus' obedience as a topic in christology the central position of the subject may cause some astonishment.

However that may be, it cannot be denied that to the question, "What was the specific feature of 'the Jesus phenomenon'?" the answer of "the principal authority, New Testament exegesis, ... in spite of many other differences, is clear: what is unique to Jesus is his unusual *freedom*".[5] The freedom of Jesus turns out to be the central christological topic in an historical and critical inquiry into Jesus, his aims and actions, his history, his effect, his person. Freedom now appears as Jesus' characteristic quality, and the one which alone makes it possible to understand in their true light phenomena such as his obedience, his doing of God's will and his acting in subordination to the divine "must" (*dei*).

If historical criticism is accepted as a method in christology, a description of Jesus' freedom is not enough. *Jesus* must be presented as "a free man" and assessed in *his* freedom. A whole range of starting-points is available in the short but rich career of Jesus, and a theological interpretation of the describable phenomena suggests itself: Jesus appears as the free man, the administrator and representative of God's freedom.

I. FREEDOM AS A THEME IN THE PREACHING OF JESUS

In the synoptic gospels the word "free" (*eleutheros*) occurs only once in the mouth of Jesus, in Mt. 17. 26, and the word "freedom" (*eleutheria*) never.[6] The story of the cleansing of the Temple (Mt. 17. 24–27), a reflection of "Jesus' relationship to the Jewish synagogues' association",[7] which presents the community as an association of the free sons of God, is a secondary tradition, but its underlying idea certainly goes back

---

[5] J. Nolte, "Die Sache Jesu und die Zukunft der Kirche. Gedanken zur Stellung von Christologie und Ekklesiologie", in F. J. Schierse (ed.), *Jesus von Nazareth* (Mainz, 1972), pp. 214–33. The quotation is from p. 218, and Nolte cites E. Käsemann, *Der Ruf der Freiheit* (Tübingen, 1968) and J. Blank, *Das Evangelium als Garantie der Freiheit* (Würzburg, 1970).

[6] Cf. Jn. 8. 32–6.

[7] W. Grundmann, *Das Evangelium nach Matthäus* (Berlin, 1968), p. 409.

to the preaching of Jesus. Even if the words "free" and "freedom" do not occur in the mouth of Jesus—perhaps the danger of being misunderstood in political terms, as a zealot, imposed a certain reticence[8]—his general approach makes freedom and the liberation of men a fundamental theme of his preaching. The imminence of the kingdom of God, which Jesus announces (Mk. 1. 15), means, for those who accept the action of God as ruler, liberation and freedom, freedom from enslavement to the rule of Satan, sin and death, freedom from social and religious pressures, freedom from the enslaving needs of an imprisoned self. It means freedom from worry which fragments the personality (and, in the best tradition of *divide et impera,* destroys freedom), from confining fear, freedom to care about God and other men, one's neighbours, fundamental personal freedom.

Jesus urged freedom on his listeners in provocative words: "Whoever would save his life will lose it" (Mk. 8. 35a); "Do not fear those who kill the body, and after that have no more that they can do" (Lk. 12. 4); "Do not be anxious about your life, what you shall eat, or about your body, what you shall put on. For life is more than food and the body than clothing. Consider the ravens: they neither sow nor reap, they have neither storehouse nor barn, and yet God feeds them. Of how much more value are you than the birds!" (Lk. 12. 22–24); "When they deliver you up, do not be anxious how you are to speak or what you are to say; for what you are to say will be given to you in that hour" (Mt. 10. 19); "Love your enemies, do good to those who hate you, bless those who curse you; pray for those who abuse you. To him who strikes you on the cheek, offer the other also; and from him who takes away your cloak do not withhold your coat as well. Give to every one who begs from you; and of him who takes away your goods do not ask them again" (Lk. 6. 27–30); "The kings of the Gentiles exercise lordship over them; and those in authority over them are called benefactors. But not so with you; rather let the greatest among you become as the youngest, and the leader as one who serves" (Lk. 22. 25–26).

[8] Cf. M. Hengel, *War Jesus Revolutionär?* (Stuttgart, 1970).

Jesus was clearly aware that "fear, hardship and threats shut the individual up in himself; he becomes closed and isolates himself from others. But egoistic or fanatical ideological aims also make people hard and closed against others, whom they may ignore and negate out of indifference, misuse and exploit as tools or, if they are in the way, label as monsters and eliminate. These socio-psychological mechanisms operate among groups and societies as well. Worry about the security of their gains (power, possessions or ideology) welds them together into tightly knit groups, which then hive off those who do not fit and are therefore dangerous (the have-nots, protestors, nonconformists) and expel them."[9] In his preaching Jesus attacked the vicious circle of unfreedom by announcing the kingdom of God to his hearers and teaching them to risk everything for its sake, urging them to be free: "Seek first the kingdom of God ... and all these things shall be yours as well" (Mt. 6. 33; cf. Lk. 12. 31).

The call to freedom is also the subject of many of Jesus' parables—a relaxed attitude in the face of clear failure (Mk. 4. 3–8), unworried confidence in the power of the kingdom of God (Mk. 4. 26–29) in spite of its invisible beginnings (Mk. 4. 30–32; Mt. 13. 33), the overcoming of religious bigotry through patience (Mt. 13. 24–30), total commitment to the unhoped for prize of the kingdom of God (Mt. 13. 44). All these are forms of the freedom of the kingdom of God. Readiness to give (Mt. 18. 21–35), approval of true, generous righteousness (Mt. 20. 1–16), untroubled investment of talents (Mt. 25. 14–30), clever dealing (Lk. 16. 1–8), even unashamed boldness (Lk. 18. 10–14) —all these are examples of the freedom into which Jesus wants to liberate men. The father in the parable of the prodigal son proclaims the freedom of the sons of God, "All that is mine is yours" (Lk. 15. 31), and invites them to the feast of life, to claim the freedom he has given them.

Jesus' preaching gives men the courage to be free. It also allows us to draw conclusions about the courage which was at the root of his freedom.

[9] H. Kessler, *Erlösung als Befreiung* (Düsseldorf, 1972), p. 69.

II. Jesus' Liberating Activity

Jesus' liberating activity is displayed most strikingly in his healings and exorcisms,[10] which also at first brought him a large following among the admiring population of Galilee. Jesus freed sick people from their sufferings—from fever (Mk. 1. 29–31), from lameness (Mk. 2. 1–12; 3. 1–6), from haemorrhages (Mk. 5. 24–34), from blindness (Mk. 10. 46–52) and other afflictions (Mk. 1: 32–34; 3. 10; 6. 53–56). His distinctive qualities included an extraordinary charismatic authority (Mk. 1. 22, 27), absolute faith (cf. Mk. 9. 14–29; 11. 22–23) and amazing freedom. "Jesus' amazing freedom had its most provocative effect on the least free of those he met, the possessed. Wherever he appeared, they went into extremes of excitement. It was often enough for him to show himself at a distance, and they would go into convulsions. Jesus regarded it as a particularly important task to heal those who were possessed by an alien force and enable them to experience the liberating dominion of God. He was not only himself free, but also led the fight against the absence of freedom in others."[11]

Anyone who can bring others to themselves must be in control of himself (and not out of his mind or possessed, as Jesus' opponents said of him, cf. Mk. 3. 20–30). Someone who can make others free must be free in a special way. Jesus interpreted his control of himself, his authority, his freedom, by reference to the Spirit of God: "If it is by the Spirit of God that I cast out demons, then the kingdom of God has come upon you" (Mt. 12. 28; Lk. 11. 20; cf. Mk. 3. 29–30). God's Spirit "possesses" him, gives him charismatic and prophetic authority, leaves its mark on his amazing freedom and inspires his liberating activity.

Another provocative aspect of Jesus' liberating activity, in addition to his healings and exorcisms, was his free association with sinners, with people who, by the prevailing standards of Jewish religion, of the piety of the time, were godless, unclean and to be avoided. Jesus grants them freedom—"Your sins are

---

[10] Cf. R. Pesch, *Jesu ureigeene Taten? Ein Beitrag zur Wunderfrage* (Freiburg, 1970).

[11] R. Schwager, *Jesus-Nachfolge (Freiburg, 1973)*, p. 40.

forgiven" (Mk. 2. 5)—frees them from their isolation by his association with them and tries to free the religious people who force them into isolation from their narrow attitudes (Mk. 2. 15–17; Lk. 15. 1–10). Jesus' freedom in this matter was felt as a scandalous pretension (Mk. 2. 7), and seemed to place a question-mark against his prophetic claims: "If this man were a prophet, he would have known who and what sort of woman this is who is touching him, for she is a sinner" (Lk 7. 39). Jesus did not ignore the scandal he caused, and did not create new scapegoats. His free demonstrations of solidarity did not set up new battle lines, but infiltrated beyond all lines. Jesus remained free in relation to everyone, and wanted to make everyone free for everyone else: "Jesus takes even his opponents seriously. He explains his behaviour and tries to make it intelligible; he listens to accusations and tries to disprove them. He does not impose conditions on anyone who wants to talk to him. A person who wants to come to him does not first have to show evidence of moral, religious, economic, cultural or political achievement. Jesus treats members of socially despised groups as his equals. By taking them seriously as partners, he removes the contempt and makes these people capable of self-respect, able to come out of the hostility of their imposed roles.

"Jesus' attitude to members of the ruling class is equally free from conditions and constraints. He shows them that it is unnecessary to hide behind privileges and defence mechanisms. Inevitably, this challenge to freedom brings conflict. A person who cannot escape from the shadow of his privileges, his position of authority, his power over others, is forced to get rid of the man who demonstrates the dangerous alternative in his own life. But Jesus' attitude enables some men to escape from their shadows, to give up their roles, to come out of themselves. These people meet, eat and drink together, get to know each other, have celebrations with Jesus, become friends. Jesus' attitude breaks down communications barriers."[12] Jesus' circle of disciples, by bringing about the reconciliation of deadly enemies, is the result of his liberating activity and the signal for a freedom movement.

[12] K. Schäfer, *Rückfrage nach der Sache Jesu* (Düsseldorf, 1970), p. 157.

There is another important part of Jesus' liberating activity, his attempt to free men from the fears that are intensified by the pressures of ritual: "There is nothing outside a man which by going into him can defile him" (Mk. 7. 15). The fear of "the unclean" is ultimately a fear of death, and it is this which drives people to set themselves apart, to keep aloof, to submit to rites. Purity regulations are a matter of life and death, and for that reason had their place in the Mosaic law.

"But the man who denies that impurity from external sources can penetrate into man's essential being is striking at the presuppositions and the plain verbal sense of the Torah and at the authority of Moses himself. Over and above that, he is striking at the presuppositions of the whole classical conception of cult with its sacrificial and expiatory system. To put this another way, he is removing the distinction (which is fundamental to the whole of ancient thought) between the *temenos*, the realm of the sacred, and the secular, and it is for this reason that he is able to consort with sinners. For Jesus, it is the heart of man which lets impurity loose upon the world. That the heart of man should become pure and free, this is the salvation of the world and the beginning of that sacrifice which is well-pleasing to God, the beginning of true worship. . . . Finally, by this saying, Jesus destroys the basis of classical demonology, which rests on the conception that man is threatened by the powers of the universe and thus at bottom fails to realize the threat offered to the universe by man himself. . . . Jesus felt himself in a position to override, with an unparalleled and sovereign freedom, the words of the Torah and the authority of Moses. This sovereign freedom not merely shakes the very foundations of Judaism and causes his death, but further, it cuts the ground from under the feet of the ancient world-view with its antithesis of sacred and profane and its demonology."[13]

Jesus no longer binds himself and his hearers slavishly to the tradition of the elders and the law, and this was the most striking demonstration of his emancipation of himself and his successors from the religious ideas of his contemporaries and

[13] E. Käsemann, "The Problem of the Historical Jesus", in *Essays on New Testament Themes* (London, 1964), pp. 39–40.

from the prevailing theology and social customs. "Since early Judaism decided that the system revealed in the Torah was the complete expression of God's covenant will, it had been inconceivable for the pious Jew that God, in his dealings with men, might not be bound by the Torah. Since the Torah was the gift of his love and mercy, his own behaviour by the rules of the Torah could not be in contradiction with love. It was true that the Torah demanded the punishment of sin, even in the life of the religious person. Nevertheless, the pious Jew regarded the Torah as the path of salvation, since on that path not only could he achieve a life ever more in conformity with God's will but he was also open to God's chastisements, by which he was, here and now, constantly purged of his guilt. . . . Jesus' opposition was directed against the way in which the prevailing interpretation of the law made it seem that laws were a way in which God made use of men for himself, for his own honour and glory. Against such interpretations of the law, Jesus proclaimed God's unconditional and unrestricted will to save, which was active in every age *for* each and every *man*. For this reason he opposed the law when it led to contempt for those who were outside the law."[14]

The independent authority of Jesus' "But I say to you" breaches the power of the dominant religion and releases men from the projections of their fears into a life in God's kingdom. Jesus binds his hearers to the freedom of love, that is, to God and their neighbour. Jesus teaches men to be good freely—*etsi Deus non daretur* (Mt. 25. 31–46). He makes God redundant as a human need, and by so doing both preserves God's sovereign freedom and inaugurates freedom for men. Jesus' liberating activity, then, establishes freedom. This allows us to say something about the authority of his freedom.

III. JESUS' FREEDOM

The courage and the authority of Jesus' freedom depend on his faith. His faith shaped his whole personality. Jesus' faith

[14] M. Limbeck, *Von der Ohnmacht des Rechts. Zur Gesetzeskritik des Neuen Testaments* (Düsseldorf, 1972), pp. 60, 83; also Limbeck, *Die Ordnung des Heils. Untersuchungen zum Gesetzesverständnis des Frühjudentums* (Düsseldorf, 1971).

gave him the authority to inspire freedom by his words and institute it by his actions. Jesus had to take first himself the decision to which he called others, to live first himself the whole existence which he helped or wanted to help them to live.[15] The instigator and founder of freedom himself lived as a free man.

Since the courage and authority of Jesus' freedom depend on his faith they are better described in terms of his faith than in terms of his relation to God. In his faith (which is most directly documented in his prayer), Jesus has a relationship with God as the Father who, in the freedom of his love, is anxious to preserve man's freedom. Jesus knows that this Father, both for God's sake and for man's, has committed him to living his life completely for others. Jesus' relationship is with God, the Father who is free to let the rain fall on both good and bad (Mk. 5. 45), to pardon godless sinners in grace and make them his friends (Mk. 2. 15–17; Lk. 15), free to interpret the law given to men in man's favour and thereby to direct man to his neighbour (Mt. 25. 31–46). This Father is free in a kindness which liberates true justice (Mt. 20. 1–6), in a spontaneity which does not wait to be asked (Lk. 15. 11–32), a patient availability, an uninsistent presence and a sovereign power which destroys the power of false powers and idols. Jesus' God "embodies grace and forgiveness, and these reappear in Jesus' assurance, superiority, openness and love".[16]

This is the psychological side of Jesus' freedom, which the sources justify us in describing as independence and superiority, distance and self-sufficiency, spontaneity of feeling and calm, relaxed cheerfulness and passionate commitment. It was also an attractive openness and a nobility which commanded respect, enormous demands combined with understanding leniency (which might look like rigorism and laxity).[17] It was in short

[15] Cf. Via, *Die Gleichnisse Jesu*, p. 191: "If Jesus interpreted his activity as God's act, the faith or view of life by which his actions and words were fed is in itself a significant dimension of God's act. The coming of the kingdom could be described as the possibility of the coming of faith in man in the sense of a coming *extra se*, i.e. as a divine act in which Jesus is a model of faith."

[16] J. Nolte, "Die Sache Jesu", p. 222.

[17] Described as such in K. Niederwimmer, *Jesus* (Göttingen, 1968).

an unusual (prophetic) confidence, the assurance of faith. "Another feature of Jesus' special freedom is openness to the real needs and interests of others. Under the name of love, this openness, in the sense of being free for others, has constantly been singled out and emphasized as 'the Jesus phenomenon', the core of his preaching, the Christian gospel in essence. This freedom's source in love and its final crucifixion marks it out from ordinary freedom. Jesus' freedom, which does not seek or defend its own freedom, but leaves itself open and free for others, breaks through the fears of a freedom sought in resentment, hatred, revenge and fear. In this way Jesus' freedom 'redeems' mankind's noblest hope—freedom."[18] Jesus' freedom can only be interpreted as the freedom of this man liberated by the Spirit of God (as God's freedom for men). Jesus' claim to possess the Spirit of God is an expression of his faith, his relationship with God, his freedom which derives from and is directed by the Spirit of God (Mt. 12.28).

To complete this picture of Jesus' freedom as human freedom liberated by the Spirit of God, we must mention a few more features which cannot fail to strike any student of the historical person of Jesus. These are his enthusiasm, his prophetic assurance, his messianic consciousness, his freedom from so many conventional restraints, his free obedience.

Jesus' preaching of the rule of God has the character of an enthusiastic proclamation. Jesus' own wonder arouses wonder, His charisma fascinates, attracts followers and releases charisms (cf. Mk. 6. 7). The source of Jesus' enthusiasm is clearly his freedom. This is revealed as a psychological factor in Jesus' characteristic unity of conscious and unconscious states of mind, in his overcoming of the conflicts with reality and authority. Jesus' "illusion" of the imminence of the kingdom of God alters reality by making it, the old world of evil, fear and judgment (the world under the rule of Satan), into a utopia (in the etymological sense of a non-existent place), a world which is passing away, for which there is no longer any room, which is being driven out by the kingdom of God (cf. Lk.

[18] J. Nolte, op. cit., p. 221.

10. 18–20).[19] Jesus solves the conflict with authority, not by suppressing it, but by altering people's conscious attitudes so that they can adopt future projections in the present and live in the future, in the Spirit, in wonder and enthusiasm. Because Jesus is free from the repressions which obscure unconscious strivings with projections, he possesses an unparalleled strength of personality. This is the source of his power to fascinate.[20]

Jesus acts with striking prophetic assurance. He is free from doubts about his mission, his programme and his path, though at the same time free in the forms he chooses to express them. His faith has made him free and capable of undivided giving. His free God, who is not bound by the law, not frozen into the role of a judge, give him an "autonomous" consciousness which harmonizes with the strivings of the unconscious for autonomy. For Jesus, the dualism of autonomy and external authority is broken because the source of authority, freedom, itself preserves autonomy. The morality preached by Jesus presupposes the reality of the new covenant in which the law of God is written on men's hearts. Jesus' realized eschatology (which, appropriately, is correctly interpreted in John's gospel) corresponds to this idea. Present and future are not to be contrasted (in projections based on the old dualism), because for Jesus the conflict has been ended by God, by the future. The announcement of the imminence and presence of God and salvation, of eschatological conversion (cf. the beatitudes in the Sermon on the Mount) can be made by Jesus with prophetic assurance because in faith he is free from doubts and lives undivided.

Jesus' messianic consciousness is similarly an expression of his freedom. He knows that he has been sent by God, and sent with a task (Mt. 2. 17) and his task is the crucial one of liberating men. Jesus can only attain an adequate understanding of his task if he sees himself as liberated, as free. In fact he does, as can be seen by the way that, even when threatened with fatal conflicts, he sticks to his determination no longer to fear God as a judge, not to look for safety in the shelter of external

[19] R. Pesch, *Von der "Praxis des Himmels". Kritische Elemente im Neuen Testament* (Graz, 1972).
[20] I owe some of the main ideas of this and the following sections to discussions with Dr Herbert Zwergel of Frankfurt.

authority (or an externally dominated society). It can be seen also in the way failure does not discourage him and death fails to terrify him. He is able to endure it in the assurance of his faith. Jesus' messianic consciousness expresses itself constantly in his preaching and behaviour as a claim and a reality. In his preaching and his actions, Jesus appears as God's representative, and the consciousness of being God's decisive agent (decisive for human freedom) marks his whole career, up to and including his death. Jesus' free and unconventional behaviour indicates that he is free from fear.

Another strong indication of this is that there is little imagery of the apocalyptic judgment imagery in his preaching. Because he has no fear, he can behave unconventionally, free from the normative pressures of society or formative relational groups. (K. Niederwimmer has emphasized his remarkable freedom from tendencies to self-depreciation or masochism.)[21] Jesus abandoned the asceticism of the disciples of John the Baptist, a group to which (as his baptism shows) he once belonged, nor does he carry out any further sacramental rites which confer a mark of immunity from the wrath of God's judgment. The basic character of his bestowal of salvation (freedom) is social communication—it is personal. Jesus defeats the legalism of the prevailing religion by pressing the Torah even further and equally by rejecting the Torah and by what was by Torah standards laxity. Jesus "did not consider himself bound by previous views. He did not take his deepest wisdom from books or oral tradition. For him things and people spoke simply by their existence. He was free from any trace of the burden of the past, and that is why he was so deeply present to others."[22]

Jesus himself interpreted his activity as determined by the will of his heavenly Father. In this, he gave his free obedience (an obedience in the Spirit who had written God's will in his heart), his words and his actions, his path (under the shadow of the divine *dei* or "must") and his death the quality of revelation. The will of the Father made Jesus' life practical revelation, which was identical with the institution of freedom.

[21] K. Niederwimmer, *Jesus*, p. 68.
[22] R. Schwager, *Jesus–Nachfolge*, p. 40.

Jesus' obedience was the acceptance of his freedom. Jesus was a free man, the free man.

IV. JESUS, A FREE MAN

"Many Christians thought for a long time—and many still think—that Jesus was not free like other men to do or not do what he himself wanted, but that he was, as it were, pre-programmed."[23] It should be clear by now that this is a false alternative. Jesus was not free like other people; he was freer to do or not do what he himself wanted, he lived in a liberated freedom, which he preached and passed on. Jesus was not pre-programmed like other people: a wider range of possibilities was open to his freedom because the institution of freedom is not a process which can be pre-programmed, but an endless task of free obedience, a task which demands inventive spontaneity, creativity, talent for innovation. His task itself made him free because it bound him completely to the cause of freedom. The "must" under the shadow of which his whole life, his journey to death, was passed (cf. Mk. 8. 31) was a tie to the will of the heavenly Father who wanted men to be free. Freedom grows at the same rate as the tie to freedom, the tie to God as the source and guarantee of freedom.

"Thomas Aquinas, in a profound insight, said that every creature in itself, 'in what it itself is, is from another'. This 'being from God' determines the nature of every creature, and the more completely a creature is 'from God' and therefore united with God, the more and the more fully it is 'itself', the more it exists in its own particularity. The hypostatic union therefore, far from excluding real 'humanity' in Jesus Christ, on the contrary implies that Christ possesses the perfection of real human existence in the highest possible degree. In other words, it implies that real humanity exists in him in a super-natural, super-human, divine-human way, that Christ is 'Man' in the way that only God can be: in Mersch's phrase 'divinely human'."[24]

[23] A comment by E. Schillebeeckx and B. van Iersel on the idea of this article in the preliminary planning for this issue.
[24] F. Malmberg, *Über den Gottmenschen* (Freiburg, 1960), pp. 45–6.

It would of course be a mistake to let this sort of dogmatic and speculative insight divert us into irrelevant speculation. Jesus was a free man and suffered death; his capacities for human suffering were not restricted. "In spite of his fearlessness he was in no sense a superman. He had all the normal human feelings. He could be pleased and inwardly rejoice. He was also liable to sadness and weariness. He even knew temptation. ... He was sometimes impatient with the people, and even with his disciples, when they refused to understand him. His nerves reacted with particular sensitivity to the thought of death. He was angry when a friend died, and at the approach of his own death he ran with sweat. Death had such power to disturb him that he would gladly have turned back in his path. It was in this moment that he displayed his unusual freedom. He could give the impulses of his body and mind free rein. He had no need to hold himself back. He was under no pressure to act tough. He could accept his trembling body and say, "Not my will, but thine, be done" (Lk. 22. 42). When he was in the hands of his opponents his silence dominated the spiteful and petty charges. Not that he maintained his position by inwardly despising his opponents—an easy thing to do in such situations. He did not become obsessed with trying to show others that they could not get rid of him. He did not rush fanatically into death like a member of a suicide squad. His own sufferings did not blind him to others."[25]

Jesus was not inhumanly super-human, and speculations about his omniscience and infallibility are beside the point. Jesus could make mistakes; there was no need for him to know everything. But we should not impute to him as a mistake something which does not fall into that category, his expectation of the end. In Jesus, expectation of the end is not a feature of an apocalyptic world-view, but part of a realized eschatology derived from his own person: "The future aspect and the present aspect of the kingdom of God are combined in the person of Jesus. For an interpretation attempting to use specific language forms to penetrate to a completely undetermined situation, this means that Jesus did not direct his hearers towards an indefinite future but introduced them into a present determined

[25] R. Schwager, op. cit., p. 42.

by God's future. In this present they were to seize the time and concentrate their strength on doing God's will now and so attaining salvation."[26]

In his expectation of the end we do not see Jesus trapped in calculations of dates. In him, it was much more an expression of his untrammelled attitude to the present which was being transformed by God's rule, the liberating change of masters. Jesus was free to do what he himself wanted because he was free from sin (cf. Heb. 4. 15), which means an absence of freedom and pre-programmes people for evil. Jesus was free to do the will of his heavenly Father—in the free obedience of the Son.[27] He could urge us to love our enemies and promise us sonship because he lived as Son in the freedom of the Father's love: "But I say to you, Love your enemies and pray for those who persecute you, so that you may be sons of your Father who is in heaven" (Mt. 5. 44).

Translated by Francis McDonagh

[26] E. Gräber, *Die Naherwartung Jesu* (Stuttgart, 1973), p. 126.
[27] See also the important article by K. Fischer, "Erlösung zum Frieden", *Orientierung* 37 (1973), pp. 80–4.

Leander Keck

The Son who creates Freedom

FREEDOM is the dominant motif in Christian theology today, as was revelation a generation ago. Restating the Christian faith in the idiom of freedom is a more complex task than merely emphasizing this aspect of salvation in order to show that the Church too is in favour of freedom. For one thing, it is no longer clear what the term "freedom" means because it has become the slogan of competing power structures. Consequently, "freedom" readily comes to mean emancipation from the opposition. Those in power see themselves to be preserving freedom, while insurrectionists see themselves to be struggling to acquire it. In such a situation, a theology of freedom easily becomes an ideology to undergird a particular group, and the enemy of freedom is invariably external. Second, the term "freedom" implies an achieved status, whereas what we know most intimately is a process towards freedom. Because a theology of freedom must be dynamic and open-ended, it may be more appropriate to use verbal nouns (liberation, emancipation). Finally, because the Christian community is implicated on all sides of current struggles for specific freedoms, Christian theology must be grounded adequately in the New Testament, the one norm acknowledged by all Christians.

We find that the vocabulary of freedom is concentrated in Paul; in the gospels it occurs rarely, and only in John 8 is it explicitly soteriological. We cannot, however, be limited to what a concordance shows, for the subject-matter (*die Sache*) appears apart from explicit terminology. The hermeneutical issue in this fact can only be identified here: How does one recognize that freedom is being illumined when the term does not appear in the text? The New Testament itself points the way, for both Paul and John interpret Jesus in terms of freedom even though Jesus himself did not discuss it. Thereby they provide precedents for ways in which one can make the meaning of Jesus for freedom explicit.

Thus we have our agenda, which we can carry out only in a suggestive way. First, we shall look at how Paul and John relate Jesus to freedom. Then we shall look at Jesus himself. Finally, we shall reflect on how Jesus creates freedom today.

I. THE INTERPRETERS: PAUL AND JOHN

With Paul, we concentrate on how he stated emancipation in Christ with regard to its scope (Romans), its predecessor in the law (Galatians) and its meaning for ethics (1 Corinthians). Such an apportionment is clearly arbitrary and a matter of convenience only.

Romans 8. 18–25 is the *locus classicus* for the scope of freedom as well as its eschatological horizon. Paul thinks within an apocalyptic perspective, according to which this age (alluded to by *to nun kairos*, v. 18), marked by suffering and bondage to corruption and death, is contrasted with the age to come. Since the present is bondage, the radical future comes as liberation, not development. Freedom of all creation is God's alternative to the present because liberation from death is the hallmark of the New Age, whose inauguration is Christ's resurrection. Christians live by that future now because they participate in Christ and receive the Spirit. Because people are part of creation, Christian existence is a pledge of the liberation of the whole creation. Creation expects the revealing of the sons of God because God's deed in Christ will not be complete until his creation is liberated.

Paul's view is not pseudo-scientific. It is rather a religious image expressing the conviction that the living God is committed to the liberation of creation from death, that this divine alternative is grounded in the freedom of God vis-à-vis the present, and that God is not the logarithmic function of trends. Paul's mythological understanding of freedom for creation should be compared with alternative mythological views, such as a cosmic catastrophe. The real question is not, is Paul's view scientifically tenable? but, which image of the future is most adequate to the nature of man and God?

For our theme, we note (a) that Paul can relate Christ's resurrection to creation's bondage to death because the "doctrine of creation" will not allow him to isolate persons from the world; (b) that radical freedom is not inherent in the present but an eschatological event, grasped now by faith and sacrament. Thus Paul relates Christ to freedom in a thoroughly *theo*logical way: liberation is the over-arching work of God.

In the Epistle to the Galatians Paul insisted that through Christ he who believes is free from the law as a way of salvation. This leads him to re-think the nature and place of the law in the "economy of salvation". The law now appears as an interim arrangement (Gal. 3. 15–20). Hence Paul speaks of the law as a "trustee" to which we are consigned virtually as "wards of the court", for a specific period of time. Under the law there is no freedom, a status indistinguishable from slavery to the elemental powers (*stoicheia*, Gal. 4. 1–11). Christ brings freedom from both. Here "law" does not mean moral law or the will of God, but religious observances as a way of salvation. By concerning themselves with observances ("days, and months, and seasons, and years", Gal. 4. 10), the Galatians unwittingly commit themselves to the law because they do not see that one cannot mix freedom in Christ with obligation to observe the law (epitomized by circumcision, Gal. 5. 2 ff.). To insist on observances is to relapse into the *status quo ante*, before Christ came; it is to deny that the law was an interim and to hold that the way of observance is permanent; it is to agree that faith is not fully competent to relate one rightly to God.

How does Paul come to reason this way? Whatever information he had about Jesus' life, he does not ground freedom in Jesus' liberating words or deeds. Paul does not disclose the steps in his reasoning; what we have is the explication of his conclusion. None the less, central considerations are clear.

Doubtless, Jesus' cross and resurrection broke open the meaning of Jesus for freedom. The crucified Jesus was indeed God's Messiah, even though, according to the law, he was cursed (Gal. 3. 13, quoting Deut. 21. 33). "Curse" is the key term: on the basis of the law, Jesus was cursed; on the basis of the same law, everyone who does not do everything required by it is also cursed (Gal. 3. 10, citing Deut. 27. 26). But if by resurrection God himself disclosed the one cursed by the law to be his son, then the validity of the law as a way to God has been terminated by God himself. Since Paul could not conclude that God contradicted himself, he inferred that the law was the great parenthesis in the history of salvation based on faith. Moreover, whoever entrusts himself to God on the basis of Jesus is rightly related to God (justified by faith) be he Jew or Gentile. If in this way the promise to Abraham is kept through this Jesus, then the "cursedness" of God's son occurred "for us" (Gal. 3. 13). To be cursed, he had to come under the law; hence "in the fullness of time, God sent forth his Son, born of woman, born under the law", so that God could "redeem those who were under the law" (Gal. 4. 4). Freedom from the law is not the result of imitating Jesus' own freedom with respect to Sabbath or kosher laws, but the consequence of the Christ-event as a whole.

Had Paul reasoned that we are free by doing as Jesus did, the law would in fact be inherently opposed to faith (or promise, Gal. 3. 21); then Jesus would have brought to light an alternative, so that one must choose between Jesus and the law. But by seeing Jesus as a God-given event, Paul can grant the validity of the law for a period of time and also insist that it is now superseded. Hence the trend in Galatia is not a shift towards a live option but a relapse into an outmoded system.

Thus Paul shows how the history of man's religiosity appears in light of the event of Christ: obligations necessary for a right relation to God are superseded. All persons are now free for God as they entrust themselves to him on the basis of Jesus' cross and resurrection.

Freedom from the law is not emancipation from obligation categorically. The core obligation is love of neighbour (Gal. 5. 14), and the first fruit of the Spirit is love (Gal. 5. 22). One maintains his freedom from law by living according to the Spirit (Gal. 5. 18). Spirit-given love opens one to his neighbour, frees to share his difficulties (Gal. 6. 2) because it emancipates from the tyranny of having to fulfil one's own desires above all (the "works of the flesh", 5. 19–21). On this basis, Paul can speak of "the law of Christ" (Gal. 6.2). Freedom is not autonomy or autarchy; rather, persons are free where Jesus is Lord, God is Father and the Spirit is the power for love.

Although 1 Corinthians as a whole interprets Christian freedom, we shall concentrate on but one point—the radical claim in 1 Cor. 6. 13 that the body is for the Lord and the Lord is for the body. Here is the centre of the ethics of freedom.

"Body" is the empirical, phenomenal self destined for freedom from death by transformation at the *parousia*. It is not the physical from which the spiritual is liberated by release.[1] Because the whole self is destined for salvation, the self is a member of Christ's body and hence subject to the Lord's claim. One must not despise the empirical, phenomenal self, nor is one's body a thing to use as one pleases, for the whole self belongs to Christ ("You are not your own; you were bought with a price. So glorify God in your bodies", 1 Cor. 6. 19 f.). If the Lord is for the body, the whole self is called to responsible life.

Paul does not envisage social or economic liberation within history; indeed, according to 1 Cor. 7. 17–31, he urges continued acceptance of the conditions of this age because they are about to be terminated anyway. In such a situation, striving to change social structures would be tantamount to making them more important than they really are. Moreover, it would imply that one's freedom is not prolepsis of God's imminent liberation of creation at the *parousia*, but the beginning of the improvement of history, and that this measurable improvement is redemption. But for Paul the criteria of freedom must not be derived from the present which has no future (1 Cor. 7. 22). However, when the end was postponed indefinitely, the demand that "everyone should remain in the state in which he was called" (1 Cor. 7. 20) readily became the banner of social conservatism. But today we distort Paul's understanding of freedom if we use 1 Cor. 7 to undermine efforts to gain social and economic freedom. For us, it is 1 Cor. 6. 13 ff. which becomes decisive. What is said here is not derived directly from the eschatological expectation but from the nature of man

---

[1] Issues relating to this fundamental duality in man's nature run through most of 1 Cor., and were probably given a gnosticizing focus by the Corinthians. But discussing these and other intricate matters concerning tendencies in Corinth must be left aside here.

and the lordship of Christ; the whole self is claimed by the Lord and placed under obligation to glorify God. Since "Body" is the means by which we are related to ourselves and to the world, Paul's axiom is the basis of a Christian ethic of freedom.

Paul discovers these dimensions of liberation because he sees Jesus' cross and resurrection as the breaking-in of the age to come when freedom will be actual for all creation. On the other hand, since John's eschatology concentrates on the present, for him liberation is not proleptic. Moreover, he can ground it in the work of Jesus even before his death because for John everything depends on acknowledging who Jesus is. Thereby freedom is linked explicitly to a particular christology. John 8. 31–8 is the basis of our comments.

John makes it clear, however, that Jesus' offer of freedom is rejected because the world (concretized by "the Jews") regards itself to be free already. Jesus' freedom is not the goal of the human quest but an intrusion which exposes the world's bondage to spurious freedom. The origin of this bondage is left unexplained, but John does indicate that its character is moral, that it has to do with human deeds and allegiances, not with man's being (finitude). Just as the world prefers darkness to light because its deeds are evil (John 3. 19), so it refuses freedom because sinning enslaves men to sin (John 8. 34). The pathos of the human dilemma is not that persons choose darkness over light, freedom over bondage, but that they deem their darkness to be light and their bondage to be freedom. Rom. 1. 21 f. suggests that Paul would have agreed.

Yet precisely because this bondage is not traced to man's finitude but to his moral life, liberation is possible now by a radical decision for the Son. He can liberate from false freedom because, as the incarnate Logos, he is the truth. As John 8 proceeds (we set aside questions of its possible strata), this alternative is restated in terms of who one's "father" is. The slaves of sin have the devil as their father, the aboriginal death-bringer and the source of lies; those liberated by the Son have God, the author of life and source of truth, as Father. The choice of one's "father" is a choice of one's ground, one's whence and whither. The devilish domain is not an "objective" alternative, as if one were faced with two gods, but is a distortion, a malign parasitic power a lie. This is why the freedom which Jesus brings is liberation for the truth. Since, for John, Jesus is the bringer of eternal life, true freedom is the gift of eternal life now.

Characteristic of John is the christological concentration of this freedom. Jesus is not the "Socratic" explicator of the nature of man's inherent freedom; were that the case, his work would be maieutic, midwifery of liberation, calling persons to actualize the freedom which is theirs by nature. Instead, like Paul, John sees freedom as *occurring* through Jesus ("Grace and truth *happened* through Jesus Christ", John 1. 17). This is why freedom is maintained only by "continuing" in Jesus' "word" (John 8. 31), which includes the meaning of the whole event not only Jesus' sayings. The discipleship mentioned in John 8. 31 differs from that of the Synoptics, where Jesus' own freedom is paradigmatic. In John, it means on-going allegiance to Jesus as the Son (John 15. 1–11 speaks of "abiding" in him), made possible by the Spirit. The disciple will experience the world's hostility because he identifies with Jesus, whom the world also rejected, but this is the consequence of freedom, not the way to it. One cannot find freedom by nurturing one's alienation from the world. That, John implies together with Paul, would merely redesign bondage because such freedom would not be derived from the Creator but from one's animosities. True freedom which the Son brings has a transcendent ground because the Son comes from the Father.

John makes Jesus state explicitly that freedom is his work. To what extent was Jesus' mission one of liberation?

II. The Liberating Event

Freedom was not a topic in Jesus' teaching. Its theme was the impingement of God's kingdom and its corollary repentance. Because Jesus neither explained the nature of freedom, nor urged it upon his hearers as a moral task, we must infer his significance for freedom from the lineaments of this mission as a whole.

To begin, the kingdom of God does not compete with human freedom. The idea that man is free only when God is dead represents the opposite view from that of Jesus, even though one must admit that churches have suppressed freedom in God's name. But Jesus articulated (by word and deed) the impingement of God's kingdom in such a way that what occurred can be called liberation. Where God is truly sovereign, there men are truly free; where Jesus was effective, there God created freedom. Because the liberating effect of God's kingly rule becomes visible first of all in Jesus himself, the person and work of Christ cannot be separated. We do not know historically how Jesus came to be grasped by the liberating rule of God; we can only acknowledge that it occurred because he was free to call the coming King "Abba" (Father), and to teach others to do so too.

Because liberation is concrete, the opening towards freedom took many forms, of which exorcism was the most dramatic. Thereby Jesus made effective the kingly power of God against the tyranny of the demonic. Healing was but a less dramatic expression of the same point. From this we infer that where God is sovereign, liberation concerns the whole person, for the God who comes as king is the creator. Stoics and Epicureans could appeal to innate, inward human freedom regardless of external circumstances; not Jesus.

Jesus' relation to the Torah shows another aspect of the liberation implicit in Jesus' work. He regarded the written Torah as an expression of the will of the same God whose kingly reign he was making effective in advance. Two consequences follow: (1) He intensified the Torah over against efforts to ameliorate its demands (e.g., the Corban saying in Mk. 7. 9–13), just as he clarified its place over against attempts to distort it (e.g., Mk. 3. 1–5. (2) The kingdom's emancipation is positive—liberation to what God wills, not emancipation from the law. Man's problem is not the Torah but its perversion. This implies that man is free, not when command is removed, but when his relation to God's will is right (when he repents). When Jesus clashed with scribes and Pharisees it was because each accused the other of misusing the Torah. So the authority of Jesus became a pivotal issue. Without any appeal to the chain of tradition, Jesus tacitly asserted that he knew definitively what was God's will because he was his "finger" (Lk. 11. 20). This is the historical basis for the Johannine insistence that the key to Jesus is his relation to the Father.

The more sharply we note the divisions of Judaism in Jesus' day, the more important is his independence from all parties and groups. Not that he was concerned only for the individual, or that he advocated a protest against the establishment. Neither his deep distrust of wealth nor his affinity for the poor are expressions of a proletarian heart. Rather they express his conviction that the coming of the kingdom would rectify all things, not consummate present trends or confirm present distributions of power. Jesus' freedom, in other words, to associate with both the poor and the wealthy, the pious and the sinners, and to share bread with the Zealot Simon and the Roman agent Levi, is the reflex of God's freedom vis-à-vis the structures of the present. Jesus refused to corroborate any group's claim to the kingdom as the divine warrant for its own expectation. This is a central element in Jesus' freedom. In short, the transcendence of God's kingly reign was not construed as its mere otherness, even less as spatial or temporal distance, but as the freedom of God to love both the sinner and the pious, the weak and the strong, in such a way that everyone's world was changed. This is why Jesus is the paradigm of freedom from the ideological use of "God" to sanction either the *status quo* or efforts to re-model it on the basis of our grievances. As the fourth gospel implies, we do not know in advance what real freedom is but discover its dimensions through Jesus.

The sovereign freedom of God to bring his kingdom made Jesus free from anxiety over human approbation. He trusted the God who sees in secret (Matt. 6. 1–18). So he was free to face even execution, though the Gethsemane story suggests that this freedom was not to be assumed but ventured. Hence Jesus did not invite persons to understand freedom or to be true to their innate freedom, but to find it by following in his way.

III. THEOLOGICAL REFLECTIONS

It was not the Jesus-tradition that taught Paul and John to speak of freedom through Jesus. Evidently they spoke of freedom because they experienced liberation as an event which occurred when they entrusted themselves to Jesus as he was presented in the gospel. Circumstances required Paul to clarify the scope of freedom against distortion, and John to defend its christocentric character. Because today we face both issues, we learn from both theologians.

We proceed differently, however. On the one hand, it is virtually impossible for us to take over directly both John's and Paul's understanding of Jesus as the incarnate form of a pre-existent being who descended to earth and then returned. Moreover, the *parousia,* and all that goes with it, is for us no longer imminent as it was for Paul. Therefore the present liberation through Jesus, emphasized by John but also found as prolepsis in Paul, is our paramount concern. On the other hand, for us the content of the name "Jesus" is irreversibly shaped by two centuries of historical studies of the gospels, so that we are drawn to the historical figure of Jesus himself.

First, we need to see the theological significance of the fact that Jesus, and his view of the kingdom, was shaped by apocalyptic. (1) Liberation does not come by managing the potentialities of the present nor by encouraging certain historical trends, but is an event which occurs as a gift, i.e., freedom is an event of God's grace. (2) Liberation does not occur without a struggle against entrenched power, whether of persons, of social structures, or of personal values and loyalties. Receiving the gift costs. (3) In this age no one is wholly free; liberators are also implicated in some form of bondage. Because they succeed only by pitting power against power, they often must cost out Beelzebul with Beelzebul. Only God-given freedom does not enslave again. (4) Because true, radical freedom is eschatological, present liberation is proleptic, and finite; it exists by faith and is an on-going process of daring to be free in the name of God's kingdom. (5) Grounding freedom in the dialectic of the "already" and the "not yet" emancipates us from idolatrous expectations of the relative freedoms which can be won through human struggle, and from an enthusiastic understanding of personal liberation as well. In history, freedom is always finite and repeatedly frustrated, but it is the only form of freedom we can experience. And it is none the less real. On the other hand, since God is indeed the true liberator, no liberation, however small or momentary, is alien to him.

Second, Jesus' all-embracing view of man implies that freedom is indivisible, and cannot be restricted to man's spirit. Nor should one insist that emancipation must begin in the inner man, or that it must begin with liberation from external social structures. One cannot contend that one must first have a successful revolution in order to free the human spirit, nor that one must first liberate the spirit before one can dismantle oppressive structures. Emancipation can begin at either point, because external and internal liberation interact with one another. Had Rosa Parks not had a measure of inner freedom she would never have refused to sit at the back of the bus in Montgomery, Alabama, and thus trigger the movement that brought Martin Luther King to prominence. Conversely, had there been no legislative emancipation, many Blacks would not have been liberated from fear in order to register to vote. Liberation grounded in Jesus pertains equally to the inner freedom of persons and to the social structures which shape the persons.

Third, Jesus makes it clear not only that freedom creates communities, but what kind of communities. Like love, freedom must be shared; it does not survive in private. But the community of freedom which Jesus inaugurated was not that of a party or sect. It was not constituted by consent to a penultimate discipline (as at Qumran) or rite (as with John's baptism) but by loyalty to the ultimate, God's kingdom. Because he opened men's lives directly to God, all sorts of persons found one another in his circle because there they were free from what before had divided them from one another. This implies, moreover, the positive meaning of freedom—freedom for one another as persons. Points of view and social structures are not abolished but are so thoroughly relativized that they no longer define who one is before God and with his brother or sister. Thus Jesus creates freedom for love without limits. The question of who is my neighbour is as inappropriate as is the question of how often shall I forgive my brother?

The community engendered by Jesus mediates the news of the Jesus-event. Thereby the community witnesses to the liberation which Jesus brought and at the same time subjects itself to the judgment of that event so that Jesus continues to liberate the Church from its tendency to forfeit its freedom.

Fourth, whoever entrusts himself to Jesus and his freedom begins to discover how and where Jesus liberates him in his own life. Paul and John show how to clarify theologically the centre and the scope of his freedom. They show how actual situations continue to provide new occasions for discovering the current frontiers where liberation must occur. Indeed, also morphology of the Jesus tradition manifests the freedom with which the early Christian communities treated the precedent of Jesus. They assumed that fidelity to Jesus permitted the tradition to be modified and expanded in order to maintain freedom in new situations. Whether the freedom brought by Jesus was always preserved in the process is another matter, one which we cannot explore here.

Finally, what is decisive about Jesus for freedom? In the first place, any answer is a confession and witness of the liberated community. But making this confession intelligible in no way establishes the decisiveness of Jesus so that someone else could make this explication the basis for his own trust. Theology does not produce commitment, though it may abet it. In the second place, the Christian community attests that Jesus is decisive because his freedom keeps on emancipating those who trust him. His freedom does not eventuate in another form of bondage; where Christians are constricted it is because they have not ventured to be as free as he made them—as Paul saw was the case in Galatia. Thirdly, the real measure of the freedom which Jesus confers is the capacity to love, for the degree to which one loves another is the degree to which one is freed from self-protection and self-aggrandizement. This boundless freedom for others is expressed in the command to love even the enemy.[2] Paul grasped the import of this freedom from self-assertion when he urged the "strong" Roman Christians to exercise their freedom to forgo flaunting their freedom in the face of the "weak" brother, just as he explained to the Corinthians that he exercised his freedom by forgoing his apostolic rights. Fourthly, Jesus' liberating power is decisive because he frees us at life's centre, the heart, where the decisive trusting occurs. That is, he frees us from false trusts and false freedoms by liberating us to trust the God of the kingdom.[3] Trusting Jesus coincides with trusting God. This is why John could make Jesus say, "If the Son shall make you free, you shall be free indeed".

[2] John's gospel, however, has no place for love of enemy, nor do the Johannine Epistles. Love appears to be concentrated on fellow believers, probably as a result of intense hostility against John's community.

[3] I have discussed trust in relation to Jesus (i.e., the Jesus discerned through critical historiography) in my book, A Future for the Historical Jesus (Nashville, 1971; London, 1972).

Walter Magass

The Price of Freedom

I

AT many places in the New Testament gospels we hear the accusation, made with remarkable bitterness, that the religious person is being provocative. The criticism is made of Jesus: "This man receives sinners and eats with them" (Lk. 15. 2). By his behaviour Jesus pays the price of freedom, the freedom of others who, as a result of the community's preventive restrictions, must stay away from the table and "away from the table" means "outside". It is one scale of values against another.

This means that a linguistic investigation using the methods of the sociology of knowledge must pay particular attention to semantic contrasts at significant points: temple and house, door and table. These are points at which men are stationed with the task of closing, to keep watch on the door and check on eligibility for the table. The examination may concentrate on hands and dishes. In their special knowledge, priests and teachers have a wide range of local criteria for "inside" and "outside". They also have explicit knowledge about admissibility to the altar or the table. On the meta-linguistic level of this biblical tradition, this includes knowledge about community, the Father's house, the forgiveness of sins, joy and table behaviour. Eating and drinking provide many lexematic starting-points for significant play-acting and models of legitimacy.

The parable of the prodigal son (Lk. 15. 11–32) is a particularly good example. In the table here we should also see one of the forms of typification by which institutions secure a hearing for, and bring order into, their interpretations of sin and righteousness. As a teacher, Jesus was not only competition for the synagogue, through his hearers who drew near and listened to him; in his teaching and behaviour at table he was also a challenge. He offered an alternative definition of reality. This involved making the market mechanism of the seating arrangements at the table public and drawing attention to behaviour at table, such as giving, taking, sharing and enjoying. We may call this series a table sequence. Our little table sequence in Lk. 15. 1–2 shows that the collision of institutions and rival legitimations indicates very accurately the price of human freedom. The signals of the conflict here are "hear" and "murmur", enjoy and murmur.[1]

The Church has kept the memory of this collision with the rabbinate alive in stories which describe Jesus' behaviour, and has in addition handed down a range of models to justify Jesus' behaviour at the story level. The same urge to justify made Jesus tell parables which included ideas that would support his table behaviour. In opposition to the experts in defining reality, he used narrative techniques in the parables to highlight a different expertise: "What man of you...?" (Lk. 15. 3). He tells a story and moulds it into a guardian of freedom. What took place in this incident between Jesus and the rabbis is that behaviour at table became an opportunity for creating an awareness of the price of human freedom, and in particular the price of the freedom of the human beings who are called "dogs" and cannot become full table companions. As it affects the price structure, the conflict of legitimations may be described as rival experts putting forward different seating patterns for the table.

The pericope of the "Canaanite woman" (Mt. 15. 21–8) illustrates some semantic contrasts which were relevant to the missionary Church in its character of an unrestricted table fellowship: between children and dogs, food and left-overs. For the stock of signs, an explosion, for the participants in the conversation a challenge to combine old and new, dignified and vulgar, in their table-talk. Whoever has the monopoly of symbols also has a monopoly in the exegesis of actions at table. Lk. 15. 2 shows that Jesus is an exegete with an undesirable exegesis. Jesus becomes a test-case. The new price structure of the larger

[1] Lk. 15. 2, 5, 9, 23.

community is not accepted. So we have one type of behaviour at table contrasted with another, and the beginning of the conflict between the communion of saints understood as the exchange of the gifts of God and men and the idea that the believer must preserve his identity even at the table, an idea which derives from the errors of possessive individualism. Both eucharistic disputes and the bread question in the more radical form it has taken since the eighteenth century derive their impetus from this table conflict between giving and keeping. Many discussions of the eucharist did not include the hunger of the children and the unrestricted table fellowship: the ministry of the altar was a reflection of the elements, bread and wine in the hands of the ministers![2] In its beginning, the unrestricted table fellowship aroused new expectations in the hungry and thirsty, which were the occasion for attacks on Jesus as "a glutton and a drunkard". God's gifts are meant to be shared, and the hungry will not be satisfied with a lesser justice at table.

The new table justice is in the background of the beatitude in Mt. 5. 6. Its effects extend to the table disasters of the Reformation period and the process of rising expectations in the revolutions of the twentieth century. Jesus mentioned God's prepared table by name: "Blessed are those who hunger and thirst for righteousness, for they shall be satisfied."

II

We turn now to the paradigms in which we shall discuss the examples which have influenced the idea of the freedom of the Church and the freedom of a Christian man. Paradigms are made by stories, especially the written versions of stories originally meant to be listened to. Studies of the history of the idea of freedom in the pre-emancipation traditions dealt mainly with the Greek analysis of freedom and the century-long discussion of *prohairesis*, which culminated in Ockham, Erasmus and Luther.[3]

Little is said about the by-ways in the history of freedom be-

[2] Yves Congar, *Lay People in the Church* (London, 1957), pp. 40–6.
[3] Walter Warnach, "Freiheit", *Historisches Wörterbuch der Philosophie* (Basle-Stuttgart, 1972) II, 1064–83; Heinrich Schlier, TDNT II, 484–500.

cause little attention is paid to the effect on the missionary expansion of the Church in the New Testament of the subsidiary meanings and overtones of the Old Testament tradition. Implicit in the whole discussion of freedom are quite specific complexes of ideas from the Old Testament. God's covenant, redemption, ransom money, sacrificial lamb and prophetic language develop into closely knit complexes of tradition with institutional contexts, and it is far from easy to bring out the complex overtones of biblical narratives and cultic language in ways which will be intelligible in modern terms.

In the areas of Old Testament tradition mentioned above, what H. Weinrich has called "spheres of images" were formed which then acted as specific motivations for freedom. In other words, the objective conditions for an awareness of freedom were created where we would least expect them, in the language of worship and meditation on worship, and in the prophetic discussions of worship and opposition to it. The distinction made by Kurt von Raumer in relation to the absolute state between corporate liberty and personal freedom needs to be worked out in terms of the various Old Testament complexes of meaning such as covenant, redemption, redeemer and price. These legitimations built up a system of services and reciprocal services which was open to inspection and which later was given shape by the literary objectification of oral acts.

Power over institutional aids, such as commandments and instructions, prayer and songs, covenant and gate liturgies, was the price of qualitative transparency for the assembled community. The system of rewards for religious actions and the price marking of God's gifts had to be clear and unambiguous. This is achieved in the *Magnificat*, and also in the pericope of Martha and Mary (Lk. 10. 38–42).

Among its various linguistic functions, worship has to provide a frame of reference for the "collective memory" (Maurice Halbwachs), since a generation's good memory is one constituent of freedom. Learning, memorizing and reciting were regarded, for instance, as one form of freedom in the synagogue.[4]

[4] Maurice Halbwachs, *La mémoire collective* (Paris, 1925); J. B. Metz, "Kirchliche Autoriät im Anspruch der Freiheitsgeschichte", in *Kirche im Prozess der Aufklärung* (Munich, 1970).

"He has established the memory of his wonderful works, the Lord who is gracious and merciful" (Ps. 111. 4). Memory must make room for wounds and negativity: "The children beg for food, but no one gives to them" (Lam. 4. 4). Among its linguistic functions, worship must keep alive an awareness of the redemption that is still to come: even the shouts and screams of "crude and tiresome agitators" about the ills of the human condition are a form of freedom.[5] In his sufferings Jesus was able to take up the tradition of the psalm as much as that of prophecy. The element of protest is an essential part of the liturgical framework and of the framework of Christian intercession for the city.

In his authority at the sickbed and at table Jesus' works of healing and his solidarity took him over the boundary of charm and into blasphemy (Mt. 9. 3). He refused to let himself be overwhelmed by the perfect criteria of the past—and that was a scandal.[6] The charge of blasphemy indicates price diffusion, a shock to the price structure of interpretation. The thoughtlessness of the interpreters leads to a collapse of prices; they offer cheap repentance and cheap grace. Altar and table lose their transparency, and so does the objective possibility of the prepared table.

Every institution places importance on the charismatic and rational transparency of its collective actions. The Christian Church has preserved Jesus' dispute with the Pharisees in the gospels as a transgression with a claim to go further. In these everyday stories of the sickbed and the table the new approach makes itself felt in style. A combination of styles is opposed to a separation of styles and Jesus begins his work in lowliness, in the deep darkness of people who have been ignored. The undiscovered everyday world is now occupied for the first time by the sign stock of a great theological tradition. Jesus has to produce arguments and he meets text with text—this is his market authority on the level of humble style (Mt. 7. 29). His method is to pile argument on argument, first proverbs from the popular stock ("Those who are well have no need of a physician"), then

[5] Cicero, de oratore III, 81: "clamatores odiosi ac molesti".
[6] Walter Magass, "Theologische Marginalien zur Provokation", in Die Strasse (Munich, 1972), pp. 76–9.

the scribal technique with a quotation from the prophet Hosea ("Mercy, not sacrifice"), and finally the ego-authority of "I came not to call the righteous, but sinners" (Mt. 9. 13).[7] On this level of humility Jesus had to pay a high price. The price is the "humble Christ" of whom Augustine speaks.

It required great efforts by the apologists and the Church Fathers to bring the "humble Christ" of the humble style of the gospels into the interpretative categories and literary canon of the old world. They brought about the adaptation by using the methods of rhetoric—appropriate, good, salutary and useful. To speak in context and to the situation was part of the pastoral approach and of the concept of pastoral freedom, "adapted to the level of the public, that is, of common sense, or of current opinion", in Roland Barthes's words.[8]

Public self-assertion in argument and refutation, doubt and demonstration, defence and disclosure, exposed the contradiction in the phenomenon of the Christian: "uneducated, common men" had authority (Acts 4. 13).

So, centuries after the Old Testament doctrine of election—"out of all the families of the earth I have chosen you alone" (Amos 3. 2)—a new paradigm of God's mercy is acted out. God did not choose an orator or a politician, but a fisherman.[9] Many of Augustine's pastoral efforts were centred in the humility of Christ. The beaten Jesus of the passion story enabled him to demonstrate the *gloria passionis*. The need to assert the humility of Jesus against the elitist spirituality of the neo-Platonist inspired North Africans forced him to analyse humility in severely realistic terms.[10]

The humble style of the gospels was for Augustine a form of freedom, freedom from a particular education: "Is there a sadder sight than that of the poor man who does not mourn for himself while he laments the death Dido suffered through her love for Aeneas?" From this point this price of humility be-

[7] Magass, *Exempla ecclesiastica, Beispiele apostolischen Marktverhaltens* (Bonn, 1972,) pp. 17–22.
[8] Roland Barthes, *Communications* 16 (1970), p. 179.
[9] St Augustine, *City of God* 18. 49; Christmas sermon 184, *Monumenta Latina* 38. 990.
[10] Erich Auerbach, *Literary Language and Its Public in Late Latin Antiquity and in the Middle Ages* (London, 1965), pp. 67–81.

came an example, a test of one's Christian vocation here below which was as valid as our perfection in glory. This is Augustine's definition of the price of freedom: "Go down in order to rise up to God. You fell when you rose up against God."[11] Apart from this tie to price, this capacity for exchange = reconciliation, the Church moved further and further into the airy heights of gnosis, in which the payments system became totally corrupt. Grace became more and more empty and reconciliation ended up costing nothing.

III

The everyday world in which we live is as system of needs and services. In the context of mutuality, Marcel Mauss speaks of a system of total services. Relationships, work, wages, sacrifice and feasts are such systems of mutuality. Into this universal mutuality language and money bring reference, qualitative difference and quantitative transparency.[12] Into these obligations of giving, taking and giving back, religion brings social coherence. Money and blood sacrifices are brought on to the level of equivalence and contrast, and similarly goats and good works (Ps. 50. 8–14; 1 Pet. 1. 18).

By sitting at table with tax collectors and sinners, Jesus exposed himself to the powerful figures of mutuality and retribution in order to reveal the ruinous circle of religious self-preservation and freedom which goes with forgetting the table. This placed him in the sphere of hands and of eye-hand images, where he was exposed to the view of others. He was seen and heard; the reciprocity of the table perspectives included him. Jesus did not want to institute a sign which made no contact with feasts and sacrifices, money, work and relationships, but wanted to pay the price of reconciliation with his presence at table.

The linguistic actions which announce this are often associated with the theme of exchange, more precisely, with spiritual exchange. In similar ways idolatry and God's kindness are trans-

[11] St Augustine, *Confessions* I. 13, 21; IV. 19; *City of God* X. 29; cf. J. Ratzinger, *Das neue Volk Gottes* (Düsseldorf, 1970).
[12] Marcel Mauss, *The Gift* (London, rev. ed., 1969).

lated into images of exchange and the call to reconciliation into the publicly transparent units of account, "blood" or expiation.[13]

The meta-linguistic level of these expressions must also take account of the objective linguistic rules of the actions. The procedures for exchanging God's gift and sacrifice/thanksgiving must be appropriate and plausible, and in particular the exchange procedures must be attached to living historical traditions to enable the pressure of history to be translated into a plausible collective action. For example, in the Deuteronomistic tradition, Israel's deliverance from Egypt is the fundamental model of God's mercies. A whole throng of acts of liberation gather round the exodus and create an infinite series of possibilities for stories of liberation. Egypt is connected with slavery and the two ideas become interchangeable. Egypt and slavery thus become free elements of action which can be linked up pragmatically with many literary themes. Conversely, God's act of liberation becomes a free element which can be linked up as a syntagmatic residue ("who redeemed you from") with Egypt, slavery, the devil, evil, Pharaoh, destruction and death, which accordingly give us the interchangeable symbols of unfreedom.

The way God's giving and taking sets a history in motion is brought out in Job's response to his sufferings. Praise of God allows him to keep a distance between himself and life, just as it allows Israel to keep a distance between itself and death: "The Lord gave, and the Lord has taken away; blessed be the name of the Lord" (Job 1. 21). In the praise of God the overproduction of symbols is so great that it exceeds the images of giving and taking and the birth-death reproduction images. This excess is the condition of freedom, which also exceeds breathing in and breathing out.

Praising God has such a superfluity of aesthetic autonomy that, even at a great historical distance, a Christian community can experience the text as an appeal. For this freedom of singing and talking the proper price to be paid by the community is worship. What looks like superfluity is in fact merely what is necessary for our common life. Songs, cries and shouts have no human price ticket, but only the fullness and grace of God.

[13] Rom. 1. 25; 3. 25; 2 Cor. 5. 18; Is. 43. 3; 52. 3.

Gertrud von le Fort says, "A thousand hours of silence are worth nothing against one song."

IV

The competition between house and Church is a prominent feature of the synoptic gospels. This becomes clear particularly in the stories of the calling of the disciples and in the commissioning scene in Mt. 12. The call to follow Jesus indicates the power of the house. Father and mother, children and wealth fall under suspicion as treasure. Following Jesus involves a change of institutions. "Everyone becomes a disciple on his own, but no one remains on his own as a disciple."[14] The slogan for laying up economic treasure is "Saving is progress, saving is strength", the Church's slogan for laying up treasure = reconciliation is "Exchange is progress, exchange is strength."

In the house-Church competition in the gospel, there are a number of signs which point either to power or to capacity for exchange. The protection offered by father, mother, brother and house is made unimportant by the richness of what Jesus gives (Mt. 19. 27-9). The rule that anyone who has power to protect also has the right to command also applies to Jesus' protection.

Table experiences with Jesus become experiences of freedom. The experience of taking, sharing and enjoying at his table make the disciples forget economic self-preservation. Church soon appears as a community of those who have understood the exchangeability of the merits of the saints and the need for exchange to produce a rapid turnover in Church actions. Giving and the ability to receive—this is the first lesson of the Christians' table experience with Jesus.

It should be noted that exchange has an emotional accompaniment, and the accompanying emotion can be a distinguishing feature. The rich young man will not take his possessions into the institutional transformation and so goes sadly on his way. In Mt. 13. 44, on the story level of the parable, the finder of the treasure enters happily into the exchange operations of selling

[14] D. Bonhoeffer, *Nachfolge* (Munich, 1961), p. 61. ET: *The Cost of Discipleship* (London, unabridged ed., 1965).

and buying. The rich young man interrupts the exchange process of discipleship, and so confirms a thesis of Marcel Mauss: "Avarice interrupts the mutually productive cycle of rights, earnings and foodstuffs."[15] What applies to self-preservation under the rules of the house also applies to the servant Jesus under God's rules. Jesus left these rules behind in order to make the seating arrangement subject to God's approval through the figure of the servant. This reversal of the master-servant relationship called in question the identity of master and freedom. For missionary strategy it became important to be able to tell stories of the humble Christ.

Even the eighteenth to twentieth century novel carries the scars of Jesus' dispossession of himself, with its important stories in humble circumstances. Service has become a ubiquitous theme.

V

In Lk. 14. 7–14, we have a table story in the style of a seating plan. The everyday world provides such a plausible pattern that seating arrangements can be used as an example. There is so much scope at the level of story that the seating arrangements can be used to justify numerous features of the Church: a Church structure with honours and banquets, polemics with the weapons of the traditional style divisions ("glutton", "drunkard" and "unfair" as insults), and finally the anticipation of eternity with its possibilities of enjoyment. The person who allocates places possesses a complex model of " higher" and "lower". In the world of symbolic meanings he controls the heavenly seating plan and the allocation of food and space. Church history as the allocation of places has still to be written. What applies to the house and the city also applies to the guardians of the bread and wine—vigilance is the price of freedom. Even today the table is a rich source of images for theology and consumption. The gifts disappear in different directions and become particles, portions, shares and spiritual gifts. Through several theological transformations the table portions are fitted into a sacrificial system, which includes spiritual sacrifice, consecration and real presence.

[15] Bonhoeffer, *Nachfolge*, p. 142.

The person who controls the bread and wine and the seating must also possess the qualities which make for good conversation at table; he must be able to tell stories. Most of them are about the founder of the table, and tell of scandal and gluttony and of the key to the distribution. Judas Iscariot and Prometheus are signals of disaster for the table. With every mouthful the old stories are present as the price of freedom and the awareness of injustice. The extent of this stock of signs is indicated by the fact that the Judas sequence of life, blood and field of blood is built on two significant texts, Jer. 32. 9 and Zech. 11. 12–13.

There is also a parable which enshrines the fact that more and more people push their way to the table and challenge the table liberties of the official guests. The tendency to go further shows itself in the invitation to the poor, the crippled, the lame and the blind. These are the people who have left the circle of social mutuality in hospitality, giving and lavish spending. What makes this unrestricted table fellowship a provocation is that these poor cannot give in return (Lk. 14. 12). This charity is disastrous for the household economy, since the house must work on the principle of at least covering costs. The parables also raise the question of price: who will look after the substance of the house if an unrestricted table is maintained? What one person devours, another must work hard to bring to the table (Lk. 15. 25–30).

VI

We shall now study the case of justification. The justification of men can be indicated by various semantic contrasts between flesh and spirit, the law and Christ, Adam and Christ and slave and free man. There are also the interpretations of the various traditions, developed for particular missionary situations. Jesus' death as currency is already part of a significant model of mutuality in interpretations such as ransom, substitution, sacrifice, expiatory sacrifice. At first sight it is hard to distinguish the semantic and pragmatic differences between these interpretations.[16]

[16] H. Conzelmann, *Theologie des Neuen Testaments* (Göttingen, 1967), p. 89.

The reinterpretations are themselves the products of syntagmatic residues ("who bought you", "who reconciled you") or traditional meaning complexes from cultic and legal rituals. Failure to see this derived character of the formulas as syntagmatic residues disorientates the hearer or reader semantically, and confuses the meta-linguistic and objective linguistic levels. This results in the introduction of status adjectives such as "true", "real" and "actual". These credit-worthy adjectives, "true", "real" and "actual", have had a field day in the Christian doctrine of redemption since the European Romantic movement. What was remarkable about this was that the doctrine of redemption was interpreted in terms of commerce, of the concept of exchange. The dealings of God and men took place within a trading community which used standardized accounting units such as services and reciprocal services. Reconciliation without a price index or method of payment is a cheat, since where there is exchange there is also cheating. In the indicative this is expressed as "God has paid the price for us". In the imperative it is "The Christian should also pay the price". When he finds the treasure in the field he enters into the transformation and sells in order to buy. The transformation includes name, work and life, which emerge as a new name, new work, etc., to indicate that exchange has taken place.[17] Jesus' life and death become relevant in terms of social significance. Currency is compared with currency, gold and silver with the blood of Christ, credit-worthiness with credit-worthiness (1 Pet. 1. 18, 19).

In a brief criticism of sacrifice, this comparison and process of going further includes a criticism of pastors and altars. The increasing quantification of the means of exchange, the wider extension of exchange relations in the market and the laying up of treasure for the house all combine to produce this suspicion, a suspicion of treasure. Similarly, Jesus' sufferings and death are not abandoned in a market based on accounting units, but for reasons of missionary strategy are interpreted in terms of the accounting units of the everyday world. Contrasts which have relevance in the market are wisdom and foolishness, lost and saved and honour and dishonour. The doctrine of redemption

---

[17] Jn 1. 42; Lk. 5. 10; 1 Pet. 2. 9; *Ling. Bibl.* 21/22, p. 7.

gives them a home and a hiding-place. Here prices are falsified or collapse, false coins circulate, and the small change of market gossip is used to pad out the text.[18] This is why down to the present we ask what silver and gold do for the city? What meaning has the costly death of Jesus for the freedom of the citizens of a city?

VII

In the Church the great table experiences with Jesus, eating and sharing at the same table with sinners, and Jesus' intentions for the table, anticipating eternity, have been translated into a liturgical system. Yesterday's provocations have become liturgical, the invitations to freedom of the table have become table controls, and bread and wine have been seen less and less as an offer of freedom. The loss of the meaning of the table has meant the disappearance of an essential dimension of Christianity. The Christian is not just a hearer of the word, but also a sharer of the bread with the brethren. Jesus' invitation to the guests who have not yet come to the table must always be remembered in the Church as a barrier against the seeping sectarian mentality, against gnosis and suspicion of bread and wine. So-called materialism and the processes of emancipation have given the suppressed questions of bread and freedom a new importance and have reminded us of Jesus' behaviour at table (Lk. 15. 2). Under this price Jesus can do nothing; the freedom of the Christian people cannot be had for less.

VIII

Excursus on the collapse of prices. Our mention of the unrestricted table community was not a reference to the Jesus of the youth movements, the escapist, the beautiful protester with the ultimate in decadent slogans: "We artists are automatic members of the kingdom of God." A hot line to God—no need for table or altar! Since Werther, Novalis and Marinetti, Jesus has been forced

---

[18] Important for a personalizing treatment is Karl Barth's *Das Geschenk der Freiheit* (Zurich, 1953), which is divided into "The Individual" and "The Event".

into a particular concept, the lonely thinker dreaming of violence and immediacy. This anti-institutional Jesus with his whip of cords in his hand is a typical figure of European youth in a certain period rather than the rabbi from Nazareth who was driven out of the synagogue.

The effect of this perspective over two hundred years must be clearly seen. The purpose of turning Jesus into an aesthetic figure is to create distance. Distance makes his presence beautiful and safe. By being taken into such objectifications Jesus will release a general feeling of well-being. Jesus Christ is thus made a free variable, and can become an epiphenomenon of cultural awakenings. Jesus' life was like a flower, said Oscar Wilde.

Christians have not been "bought" with the blood of Jesus for an elegant life in freedom, but to be a people for Jesus' possession, a people "zealous for good deeds" (Tit. 2. 14). Jesus' life did not conceal the means of our liberation and did not shrink from economic activity and the ability to exchange! He did not settle for the dandy freedom to live and die in front of one's mirror. The commercialized Jesus comes with the claim to be modern. The records offered for sale are the sign of a self-presentation and reconciliation which costs nothing, or very little.

IX

The price of the freedom of the table is Jesus' fight for places for Levi and the 5000. In the text performance the form of the series—taking, thanking, breaking, giving for them to give to the people—is a table liturgy in which Jesus and his table companions take part. The sequence should be studied (Mt. 14. 19). This sequence has become part of many forms of distribution in the course of history. The calculating approach to the table, which hesitates to talk to others or to accept, was for Jesus a provocation. Scandal starts with sharing, with the exchange of gifts. Solidarity, participation and happiness attach themselves, as significant "neighbours" of the word, to the reworking of the freedom of the table in the text. Even the left-overs, scraps and fragments are important for having one's fill of bread and fixing its price. Such literary trifles (Russian *melotch*) as scraps of bread and scraps of clothing have grown right out of their messianic framework and have created their own stories and become institutions of the Church. The crumbs from the table turn into a provocation for the woman, who must ask and beg, and so become paradigmatic for the new missionary situation. The collecting of the crumbs serves the freedom of many people.

The parables and the liturgy of the Church have taken over the paradigm of "sacred trading" as an interpretation of the liturgy. The individualistic atheism which refuses all table experiences has for centuries been providing new models of disaster for the table: not talking to people or sharing and eating with them. This has often been done under the slogan "Getting away from people to God". Jesus paid for this arrogance. That is why the Christian Church keeps a memory alive, the memory of suffering. Places at the table continue to be important. They are the shape taken by freedom to build a community which needs and is capable of exchange.[19]

Translated by Francis McDonagh

[19] Jost Trier, *Reihendienst* (Münster, 1957).

Nicholas Lash

The Church and Christ's Freedom

"IF YOU continue in my word, you are truly my disciples, and you will know the truth, and the truth will make you free" (John 8. 31–32). According to that promise, truth is discovered by dwelling in Christ's word; and the truth that is thus discovered is a truth that liberates.[1] The Church is the community of those who seek to "hear the word of God and do it" (Luke 8. 21). We could go on from here and assert that the Church, the community of Christian belief, expresses, embodies and proclaims man's freedom in God.

But would such an assertion be true? Many people would unhesitatingly answer no. They would say that the Church is too deeply enmeshed in a web, woven by history, which has irredeemably entwined its structures and attitudes with just those economic, social and political forces which, at least on a world scale, stifle or inhibit man's search for freedom. Moreover, if men are to be freed, they must be enabled critically to confront, and come to grips with, the roots of their alienation; whereas Christian preaching and worship are characteristically ideological, and thus effectively distract men from the task of liberation. In other words, the Church, in its structures and in its consciousness, masks rather than expresses, frustrates rather than embodies,

---

[1] In recent theological discussion, the concept of liberation has tended to acquire a rather technical and precise sense. In this article, unless the context indicates otherwise, I am using it more generally, to refer to the result as well as the process. Similarly, I am using the concept of freedom to refer to the process ("freeing", "being freed") as well as the result.

denies rather than proclaims, the freedom of man, the freedom of the sons of God.

Others would, equally unhesitatingly, answer yes. The freedom of which the gospel speaks is interior, religious, eschatological. And of *this* freedom the Church, the community of Christian belief, continues to be both an expression and an embodiment. Salvation is found in the Church.

It is tempting to generalize, and to suggest that the most fundamental line of division separating Christians today is drawn between the two types of answer that I have sketched. But it is impossible to know whether my original assertion is true or false, and in what sense and within what limits, unless we know what that assertion means. My initial concern, therefore, is the modest one of trying to throw some light on what it might mean to assert that the Church expresses, embodies and proclaims man's freedom in God.

I. Freedom and Salvation

What do we mean by "man's freedom"? John Robinson has remarked that, if you try to "net" the concept of freedom "in the categories of discursive knowledge, let along capture it in a verbal definition ... it slips through your fingers, and you end up, as deterministic philosophies do, by concluding that it does not exist".[2] Let me, therefore, shift the emphasis: what do *we* mean by 'man's freedom'? We (the community whose bond of discourse is successive issues of *Concilium*) are Christian men and women. Therefore, in asking questions about freedom, we are asking questions about *human* freedom, because we are men and women. We are asking questions about *Christian* freedom, because we are men and women who seek to interpret their existence in the light of the mystery of Christ.

Are these *two* freedoms? And, if so, how are they related one to another? Are they two names for one single freedom? And, if so, what distinctive contribution might we be expected to make, as Christians, to the expression and embodiment of this one freedom of man? Such questions are, of course, ultimately chris-

[2] J. A. T. Robinson, *Christian Freedom in a Permissive Society* (London, 1970), p. ix.

tological, as their form indicates. (Indeed, for some theologians, the concept of freedom is the defining centre of their christology.)[3]

When, in our search for the meaning of Christian freedom, we turn to the Scriptures, we find ourselves caught up in a cluster of methodological and hermeneutical problems. Thus, if we were to assume that there is a more or less one-to-one correspondence between our contemporary concepts and their nearest terminological equivalents in the Scriptures (a bizarre assumption, but one not uncommonly made), then we would investigate the connotations of the concept of "freedom" in the Old and New Testaments. We should find that the words "free" and "freedom" are almost always used, in the New Testament, only in a theological sense which is not, as such, directly based upon the Old Testament, but which seems rather to reflect Greek usage in the secular culture in which the New Testament was born.

Amongst the biblical concepts or families of concepts whose range of meaning closely corresponds to modern concepts of "freedom" and "liberation", that of "salvation" is of particular interest. The Hebrew root whose derivatives are usually translated by "salvation" and cognate terms seems primarily to refer to "the possession of [living] space and the freedom and security which is gained by the removal of constriction".[4] Hence, in the pre-exilic period, the concept of salvation is that of military victory, and of rescue and liberation from *any* trouble—from foreign domination, from poverty, from illness. After the exile, an increasing emphasis on the future, and a deepening messianic hope, gave a new note of ultimacy to the concept. It now acquired overtones of total, unshakeable, everlasting victory and liberation for God's people. Thus the concept of salvation "approaches the idea of liberation from all evil, collective and personal, and the acquisition of complete security"[5] and peace.

From the point of view of the problems with which I am concerned here, it is of fundamental importance to notice that the Old Testament concept of salvation is a theological concept in the sense that, for the Hebrew, all victory and liberation from evil,

---

[3] Cf. P. Van Buren, *The Secular Meaning of the Gospel* (London, 1963).
[4] J. L. McKenzie, *Dictionary of the Bible* (London, 1966), p. 760.
[5] McKenzie, *op. cit.*, p. 761.

collective or individual, present or future, is ascribed to the activity of God, to the God who sets his people free.

In the New Testament, the same cluster of meanings are retained but now, under the influence of the Greek words chosen to express the biblical concept, "salvation" acquires new overtones of healing, wholeness, well-being, health. The frame of discourse within which the concept is employed is one in which considerable emphasis is placed on the ultimacy, the finality of the salvation wrought by God in Christ. There is also, in contrast to the Old Testament, a marked concentration on the individual, "interior" aspects of salvation: salvation as "seeing", for example, or as "hearing". But these are shifts of emphasis, surely, not a rejection of the broader frame of reference which characterized the Old Testament context. Even in its final New Testament usage, the concept of salvation still retains the resonances acquired during its long history. In other words, the concept of salvation in the New Testament is a theological concept in the sense that liberation from all evil, collective or individual, present or future, is ascribed to the activity of God in Christ.

It could be objected that the point which these preliminary observations have been concerned to make might have been more succinctly expressed in Aquinas's phrase: *Omnia autem tractantur in sacra doctrina sub ratione Dei.*[6] This is true, but all of us, Catholics and Protestants, are heirs of centuries of Christian schizophrenia which has encouraged us continually to lose sight of, or explicitly to deny, the significance of that *Omnia.* We are not doubly enslaved and doubly freed. There is not economic, political, psychological slavery and also the slavery of sin. There is not economic, political, psychological freedom and also the freedom with which Christ has set us free. The slavery and freedom of which politicians, economists, sociologists and psychiatrists speak is the slavery and freedom of which Christian preaching and theology speak. The latter, however, have the specific responsibility of speaking of this human freedom, of each and every human freedom, *sub ratione Dei.* With this in mind, let us now return to the assertion with which we began.

The Church, the community of Christian belief, expresses, em-

6 *Summa Theologiae,* Ia. 1, 7.

bodies and proclaims man's freedom in God. Is this assertion true? It is true that the Church has never lost sight of the fact that its fundamental duty is to proclaim and to embody the liberation, the healing and the salvation of man by God. But, if I am correct in suggesting that the concept of salvation, the Christian concept of freedom, is a theological concept in the sense that, to Christian faith, all liberation from all evil is ascribed to the activity of God in Christ, then it is also true that the Church has frequently misunderstood this duty. It has frequently spoken and acted as if its responsibility were, not to speak of human freedom *sub ratione Dei*, but to speak of some other freedom only obscurely and tangentially related to that freedom for which we hope, for which we work, and which we partially and incipiently experience, as human beings. At best, the Church has frequently spoken and acted as if its only concern was with the interior, psychological or moral aspects of the freedom of the individual or as if its only duty, in the midst of human slavery, was to proclaim that, in the end, beyond the end of time, man will be fully free.

"Equality", said Hegel, "was a principle with the early Christians; the slave was the brother of his owner.... This theory, to be sure, has been retained in all its comprehensiveness, but with the clever addition that it is in the eyes of Heaven that all men are equal.... For this reason, it receives no further notice in this earthly life."[7] Something similar is the case in respect of the Christian proclamation of salvation. By means of the "clever addition" we have been led to misconceive the sense in which salvation, liberation or freedom are "theological concepts". As a result, the extent to which the Church has, in practice, been concerned effectively to express, embody and proclaim the freedom of man has been dramatically restricted.

It does not follow that the rejection of our initial assertion as false (a rejection which I outlined at the beginning of this article) can be endorsed without qualification. It would be historically absurd to deny the contribution which Christianity has made, and continues to make, to the liberation, the freeing, the healing, the hoping, of man—both collectively and individually. Never-

[7] G. W. F. Hegel, *Early Theological Writings* (Philadelphia, 1971), pp. 88-9.

theless, if we are really to meet the challenge with which the contemporary rejection of the community of the Church confronts us, we must face up to the implications of the fact that the critics of "institutional Christianity" are, increasingly, men and women whose deepest human and Christian hope is that the Church might, convincingly and effectively, express, embody and proclaim man's freedom in God. The enemies of the gospel do not criticize the Church. They ignore it.

II. THE CHURCH AND MAN'S FREEDOM

It is from Christ that the Church draws its life, its meaning and its power. The Church, in so far as it *is* the Church, lives by the Spirit of the risen Christ. If we ask, therefore, how the Church might less inadequately discharge its responsibility to express, embody and proclaim man's freedom in God, we are asking about the relationship between Christian freedom, today, and the freedom of Christ. By reflecting on that relationship we can also cast some light on a question which was touched on earlier, namely: what distinctive contribution might we be expected to make, as Christians, to the freedom of man?

From the perspective within which this article is written, the fundamental structure of the Church's relationship to Jesus may most conveniently be expressed in terms of *remembrance*.[8] We "continue in his word" to the extent that we faithfully hear that word and do it. The freedom for which we work and hope will be that freedom which *he* expressed, embodied and proclaimed, only in the measure that we succeed in "remembering" his freedom faithfully, without distortion or diminution.

At this point, the theologian is tempted to indulge in some purely formal, "theological" discussion of the nature of such "remembrance". And this, in the twentieth century, he may not do. We cannot evade the implications of what Peter Berger has

---

[8] This statement should not be understood as if my intention were reductionist. There are other aspects of the Church's relationship to Jesus the examination of which would demand the use of other models. Thus, for example, I wholeheartedly endorse the insistence on the inescapable function of ontological considerations in christology expressed in D. M. MacKinnon, "Substance in Christology—a Cross-Bench View", *Christ, Faith and History*, ed. S. W. Sykes and J. P. Clayton (Cambridge, 1972).

described as the "root proposition" of the sociology of knowledge, a proposition derived from Marx; namely, that "man's consciousness is determined by his social being".[9] How are we to ensure that our remembering of Jesus, which will determine our understanding of the freedom for which we seek, is not an illusion; that it is consciousness, and not false consciousness? If we brush this problem to one side, then our Christian self-understanding (and thus also our preaching and theology) will be ideological.[10] As such it will, in the long run, contribute not to the freedom of man, but to the perpetuation of his enslavement.

In any society, existing social structures, beliefs and attitudes are strengthened and legitimated in so far as it can plausibly be maintained that things have ever been thus, and that the way things are is, fundamentally, the way that God wills them to be.[11] Thus, for example, when received notions of "salvation" are challenged, the challenge is likely to be resisted on the grounds that the alternative account offered is "untraditional" or "unbiblical". This may, indeed, turn out to be the case. But it is just as likely that the fundamental ground of the resistance is the threat which the challenge poses to existing structures, practices, self-understanding and identity. Beneath the battle of words in theological debate there is often a deeper struggle engaged, of which the participants may well be unaware. Moreover, it is important not to lose sight of the fact that the process of legitimation is necessary for the social transmission of beliefs, attitudes and values. We may, indeed, be obliged critically to question our legitimations but, in doing so, we cannot afford to lose sight of the risk involved; the risk, that is, of destroying the social cohesion, and hence existence, of the very belief-system which we seek to "correct", to "purify" or to "reform".

Habermas has argued that the basic concern which animates man in his historical search for survival, for life, for fulfilment, is his quest for emancipation. Man seeks liberation from every-

---

[9] P. L. Berger and T. Luckmann, *The Social Construction of Reality* (London, 1971), p. 17.

[10] Cf. P. Fransen, "Unity and Confessional Statements", *Bijdragen* 33 (1972), pp. 29–30, discussing recent developments in the thought of J. B. Metz.

[11] Cf. P. L. Berger, *The Social Reality of Religion* (London, 1973), pp. 38–60.

thing that limits, constricts and oppresses him. Human history is the history of man's search for freedom, for salvation. This search for freedom finds expression in the quest for control over the environment (man the worker, the natural scientist, the technologist); in man's attempt to situate himself within the linguistic, cultural tradition from which he springs (man the storyteller, the historian, the exegete); and in his quest for some measure of wholeness, of identity, in a world of bewildering complexity, fragile meaning and endemic insecurity (man the constructor of social institutions). The human species thus secures its existence in systems of social labour and self-assertion through struggle, through tradition-bound social life in ordinary language communication, and with the aid of ego identities that at every level of individuation reconsolidate the consciousness of the individual in relation to the norms of the group.[12] Sociologically, the respective achievements of these three aspects of mankind's search for existence, and for emancipation, "become part of the productive forces accumulated by a society, the cultural tradition through which a society interprets itself, and the legitimations that a society accepts or criticizes".[13]

If, as I have suggested, the relationship between the Church and Jesus is fundamentally one of *anamnesis*, of remembrance, then it is clear that the aspect which most immediately concerns us here is that of the "cultural tradition through which a society interprets itself". Before taking up again our discussion of the structure of remembrance, however, it may be useful briefly to consider the relationship between this aspect and the other two.

The hard-won and fragile identity and security achieved by legitimation, whether religious or secular, is itself a form of freedom—a freedom from insecurity, meaninglessness and anarchy. But the partial and particular nature of the achievement also renders it, inevitably, a form of *un*freedom. (Nowadays, we hardly need to be reminded, for example, of the ambivalence intrinsic to the notion of "law and order".) As such, it is questioned and threatened, as I suggested earlier, by the achievements of the hermeneutical quest to liberate man from the restrictions of the

[12] Cf. J. Habermas, *Knowledge and Human Interests*, trans. J. J. Shapiro (London, 1972), p. 313.
[13] *Ibid.*

present moment through the critical reappropriation of his for-gotten past. In the Christian context, this task of critical reappro-priation is the task of attempting, more faithfully and concretely, to "remember Jesus".

Thus Habermas, who remarks that "The same configurations that drive the individual to neurosis move society to establish institutions",[14] describes the characteristic epistemological concern of the hermeneutical sciences in terms of analogies drawn from Freudian psychotherapy. The patient is "liberated" by coming to terms with, by "remembering", his buried past.

If we reflect, therefore, on the inevitable tension between these two distinct aspects of man's quest for freedom, it becomes clearer why the Church may never become simply a revolutionary force, or simply an endorsement of the *status quo*. As a human institution, the Church seeks that form of freedom which is security, identity, order, here and now.[15] As an historical people, a people constituted by the language it has inherited, the Church seeks to liberate itself from the restrictions which the past has imposed upon the present, by seeking ever more faithfully to "hear" the message that gave it birth. In the measure that it succeeds in so doing, it will discover the courage to be free for the future: to be effectively critical of its own ideological dimen-sion, of its own institutionality, and of all other partial, particular present achievements of human freedom, individual and social.

The relationship between the task of remembrance and man's quest for freedom through instrumental knowledge and control may be more briefly stated, although it is here that confusions concerning the relationship between "religion" and "politics" characteristically arise.

The Christian community cannot fail to be concerned with man's quest for liberation through instrumental knowledge be-cause that community exists in order to express, embody and proclaim man's freedom in God. In so far as it is concerned with man's freedom, the Church is necessarily concerned with his freedom through work, through scientific discovery, through

[14] *Op. cit.*, p. 276.
[15] Cf. E. Schillebeeckx's remarks on the Church's responsibility for the individual, in "Critical Theories and Christian Political Commitment", *Concilium*, April 1973 (American edn., Vol. 84).

economic and technological development. Yet, in so far as it is concerned, not simply with this or that particular form of man's freedom, but also, beyond these particular forms, with man's total, ultimate, eschatological freedom in God, the Church will be critical of the tendency to reduce the quest for freedom to its instrumental dimension. Thus, on the one hand, the Church will proclaim man's right to work and to share in the fruits of his labour. On the other hand, it will proclaim that man does not live by bread alone.

III. REMEMBERING CHRIST'S FREEDOM

How is the Church to remember Jesus? Specifically, how is the Church more faithfully to remember the freedom of Christ, that freedom which the Church seeks to express, embody and proclaim in its celebration of the resurrection of Jesus Christ? In the answer to this question lies the clue to the distinctive contribution which Christians might bring to man's manifold quest for freedom. At the same time, the answer given in practice to this question will determine the stance which the Church adopts in respect of man's quest for freedom through instrumental knowledge and through social legitimations.

Our previous discussion has already ruled out one answer to this question. The task of faithfully remembering the freedom of Christ cannot be executed at the level of theory alone. Biblical exegesis, historical inquiry, theological reflection are certainly not unimportant, but neither are they adequate to the task. They are inadequate because, at any given period, it is precisely the unrecognized limitations and deformations, imposed on the consciousness of Christians by their history, from which they need liberation.

The form of the Church's quest to remember the freedom of Christ cannot, then, be merely theoretical. It must be a practical form of life, and not merely a form of words. Where any relationship between individuals, or groups of individuals, is concerned, the attempt to move from mutual ignorance to mutual understanding, or from disagreement to agreement, is doomed to failure if it is restricted to a search for common statements or common concepts. If we would really understand the other

person, we have to come to share the experience which determined the horizon within which his beliefs and attitudes took
shape. Nor is it sufficient if the attempt to share the experience
of others is restricted to an effort of the imagination. (The rich
may make valiant imaginative efforts to share the experience of
the poor, but this will not take them far enough.) In order to
understand others, in any concreteness and depth, it is necessary
in some measure to try to do what they did, to live what they
lived. Only in the measure that we succeed, shall we then be able
to hear what they heard, and to say what they said. Conceptual
agreement is the conclusion, not the premise, of the search for
understanding.

In order less inadequately to remember Christ's freedom, thus
enabling his freedom to set us free, the community of the Church
has to have the courage to risk doing the truth in love without
waiting for the resolution of complex theoretical and hermeneutical problems.

This is not to suggest that the Church's continual attempt to
remember Christ's freedom, the Church's quest to allow itself to
be freed by that freedom, demands a programme of mindless
activism. Responsible practice is not mindless. To question the
primacy of the theoretical in the concrete enterprise of remembering the past is not to suggest that this enterprise can be under-
taken without words or images. But the words and images that
we use, and the way that we use them, will perhaps have more in
common with the use of poetry than with the elaboration of theory.
(To repeat: it is not a question of denigrating the role of theoretical reflection, but of acknowledging that it is derivative and
second-order in respect of concrete living and loving, hoping and
speaking.)

What is it which makes a *people*, over and above its information and practical know-how, its institutions and customs? At
the deepest level there will be found a cluster of images, symbols,
words and silences, in the evocation and shared use of which a
people discovers and sustains its identity, its specificity, its hopes
and plans.[16] This is no new insight of the sociology of knowledge; it kept the people of the old covenant alive in their cele-

[16] Cf. P. Jacquemont, J.-P. Jossua, B. Quelquejeu, *Une Foi Exposée*
(Paris, 1973), p. 121.

bration and their remembering or their re-living of liberation from Egypt; it keeps the people of the new covenant alive in their celebration, their remembering, their re-living of the freedom of Christ—of that act of liberation in the past which sets us free, in the present, to make our specifically Christian contribution to the promised ultimate freedom of man in the future.

If the Church is less inadequately to express, embody and proclaim the freedom of man in God, it urgently needs a deepening of that poetic consciousness which is its power to evoke and to sustain the deep symbols and silences that give it life and identity. Paradoxically, if the Church is to perform, with greater efficacy and vigour, its supportive and critical roles in respect of the instrumental and institutional aspects of human freedom, what it most deeply needs are those apparently "useless" people, the poets and prophets who sing the songs of freedom.

It was in a context of celebration, of common worship, that Jesus evoked the people's memory of liberation in order to proclaim, in the accents of human freedom, that ultimate freedom of man in God which his life and death signified and proleptically achieved: in the synagogue, "He stood up to read, and . . . found the place where it is written: 'The Spirit of the Lord is upon me. . . . He has anointed me to preach the good news to the poor. He has sent me to proclaim release to captives and recovery of sight to the blind, to set at liberty those who are oppressed. . . . Today, this scripture has been fulfilled in your hearing" (Luke 4. 17–21).

Edward Schillebeeckx

The "God of Jesus" and the "Jesus of God"

THE New Testament contains the testimony of men who found salvation explicitly from God in Jesus of Nazareth and who therefore called Jesus, in the light of their expectations of salvation and confronted with his concrete historical appearance in history, "the Christ, Son of God, our Lord".

I. THE HISTORY OF SUFFERING: MAN'S EXPECTATION OF SALVATION

Man's ideas and expectations of salvation and of personal and social happiness have always been formulated in the light of his experience of and reflections about the absence of salvation, suffering, misery and alienation. They have, in other words, arisen from an accumulation of negative experiences throughout a history of suffering that has lasted for centuries. This history, however, has always included fragmentary experiences of happiness and the promise of happiness, of salvation and of unfulfilled expectations, mingled with experiences of guilt and evil. This, of course, is the problem of Job in human history.

What has eventually emerged from this experience and man's reflection about it is a view of what is good, happy and true in the state of being man. Man's longing for happiness and salvation, which has always been subjected to criticism, but which has always survived that criticism, has therefore developed into the idea of redemption or liberation *from* and of going *into* a completely new world. This fundamental idea has, of course, been expressed in many different ways, but it is in general true to say that a people's negative experiences of contrast mark out its ideas and expectations of salvation. It is so to speak possible to read the history of a people's suffering in its expectation of salvation even if the precise traces of that suffering cannot be followed in other sources.

Jesus' own period of history was marked by a proliferation, among both the Jews and the Gentiles, of expectations of salvation and these were expressed in a full spectrum of ideas which had accumulated in centuries of historically experienced salvation and of unfulfilled expectations. The Jewish apocalyptic period, from the Maccabees (167 B.C.) through the Jewish war (A.D. 66–70) to Bar Cochba (A.D. 135), was above all a "history of blood and tears",[1] which gave rise to an increasing longing for a definitive and radical change in the world.

Within this sphere of general expectations, within which many of the ideas of salvation merged together, the conviction grew, in confrontation with Jesus of Nazareth, that there was "salvation in no one else" (Acts 4. 12). The early Christians expressed their experience of salvation from God in Jesus in ideas which already existed for them and which had been derived from many sources, but which they vitally shared. They believed that their expectations had been fulfilled here and now in Jesus of Nazareth and that they were consequently new men.

After a period of Christian life and reflection, these early believers bore witness, in the New Testament, to their recognition of their salvation in Jesus. It is not possible, however, to disentangle the closely interwoven threads of their expectation of salvation and their happy recognition of the fulfilment of that expectation in Jesus of Nazareth that are found in the New Testament. The question about man's true being and the finding of an answer to this question in the historical man Jesus are correlative. They are, moreover, correlative in that it is not the already existing expectations of salvation that determine who Jesus is, but that, in the light of the history of Jesus, those expectations are not only included, but also changed, adapted or corrected. There is, then, both a continuity and a discontinuity between man's ques-

[1] M. Hengel, *Judentum und Hellenismus* (Tübingen, [2]1973), p. 354.

tion about salvation and the concrete historical answer which is Jesus.

This means that we encounter great difficulties when we read the New Testament for the first time. We do not live in a social and religious environment with a traditional expectation of a Messiah or a mysterious Son of Man or of the approaching end of the world. We are, in other words, confronted in the New Testament with an early religious society, which is very strange to us today, both in its Jewish and in its Hellenistic expressions of these expectations. Such expectations are always conditioned both historically and culturally, even though the "human predicament" may remain the same.

In the modern world, man's expectation of salvation has assumed the form of a movement of "emancipative freedom". The aim of all the branches of this movement is to redeem mankind from his social alienations. At the same time, many different kinds of scientific techniques, such as psychoanalysis, Gestalt therapy, social work, counselling, and so on, are used to liberate individuals from personal alienations and from a loss of personal identity. A conviction which has become more and more widespread nowadays and which is increasingly used as evidence is that, apart from Jesus, there are so many factors in man's life which really bring historical salvation and make man whole. The expression, "there is salvation in no one else" other than Jesus Christ, so often used by Christians, has therefore become to some extent difficult to understand and to believe. The religious concept of salvation has undoubtedly become narrower in the modern world and it has had to give way to other and visibly effective means of bringing salvation. This has brought the question as to what really saves man into a position of central importance.

It is certainly true that it is possible to eliminate all kinds of human alienations by scientific and technical means. At the same time, however, the only alienations that can be removed in this way are those which result from the presence of physical or psychosomatic conditioning or conditioning by social structures, from the absence of conditioning by infrastructures or of liberating conditions or from the presence of conditioning by freedom that can be helped by human commitment. Human freedom is not, after all, a purely inner freedom. It is physically directed outwards and can only become fully conscious of itself when it encounters free people within structures that make freedom possible.

Man himself is only a possibility of freedom and freedom itself is really a vacuum and without content. Society enables freedom to fill that vacuum creatively, although there is no form or degree of society that can completely fill the vacuum. The individual person, society and "nature" are related to each other in a situation of dialectical tension, with the result that the deepest human alienations can never be fully overcome, either personally or socially. There is, for example, that human suffering which cannot be resolved by social or political measures. Man can still be broken by isolation even in the best social structures, since these cannot automatically make man and society good and mature. Nature can be humanized to a very great degree, but it will always remain alien to man (death is an example of this). Finally, man's finite nature may make him trust in God or it may lead to isolation and anxiety. Within human history, then, and in confrontation with nature and these various data, there is no single identifiable subject which can bring about man's total salvation or a state of real "wholeness" in him. Everything is, in fact, subject to the dialectical tension that exists between the person, society and nature.

Is this deeper problem, then, not expressed in a specific way in Jesus of Nazareth (as in all religiosity)? For slaves, salvation is emancipation. For the man who believes that his life is determined by an arbitrary fate or by evil powers, salvation is achieved in the overcoming of that fate or those powers. The material content of the "Good News", the gospel and salvation, for us changes according to our experience of the absence of salvation. It is clear from the history of Christianity since the time of the early Church that the material content of this Good News of salvation experienced in Jesus has been described in constantly changing forms, a process which is continuing for us.

Both our own longing for salvation today and what was expressed in Jesus make an essential contribution to our formulation of an answer that is faithful to Jesus and at the same time applies to us. The offer of salvation from God in Jesus will therefore subject our longing for salvation to criticism. Is it, then, not those alienations which cannot be removed by scientific and technical means used by man that are expressed in our interpretation of life as Christians in Jesus? If this is so, then it means that these human factors are recognized, confirmed and stimulated as such in this religious interpretation of reality, which has the essential task of liberating man from his deeper alienations and of redeeming him and setting him free so that he becomes autonomous in his adherence to the living God who is transcendent and can therefore make him free.

Man's search for the message and the praxis of Jesus of Nazareth is therefore a search for the structures of what appears in Jesus as really "Good News" in the religious and human sense. It is not therefore a search for confirmation of what we, as men, can probably already achieve ourselves in the scientific and technical sense. However meaningful and indeed necessary it may be, this scientific and technical skill is not, for twentieth-century man, "Good News" from God (see Mark 1. 14–15).

II. The Question about God and the Question about Man

In the light of what has been said above, it should be clear that Jesus cannot give a universal invitation that is justified by the consent that we give to it in faith, so long as it is not meaningfully demonstrated that we are essentially concerned here, in the man Jesus of Nazareth, with the living God as the creator of heaven and earth who makes us free and at the same time gives meaning to our lives. If the living God, the God of Jews, Muslims, Buddhists, and so many others, is not personally involved in the event of Jesus and does not allow his face to be seen in one way or another in Jesus, then our enthusiasm for Jesus as a man who can inspire and give direction to our lives may well be meaningful, at least within the limited tradition within which he appeared, but it will be non-committed and at the most a cipher for man's possibilities. This may still be inspiring, but it cannot be universally valid.

In his historical appearance, Jesus becomes a renewed and deepened question for us only if and because he is the one who has something definite and definitive to say about God and at the same time about man. In other words, he becomes a question if

God is expressed in Jesus as a challenge to man. Within this question, what has to be sought in Jesus of Nazareth is the possibility of signs which may be able to direct man's question about salvation towards the Christian offer of an answer in faith which will point to God's special saving activity in Jesus of Nazareth, an activity that can be identified as such by Christians. The answer to the question about the unique and universal significance of Jesus will therefore inevitably be connected with the revelation, on the one hand, of God's true face and, on the other, of man's true face, in which God's own face becomes to some extent evident and visible.

The question regarding the unique and universal significance of Jesus (as postulated by Christianity) can, of course, only be answered in faith. Any such theological statements made in faith must, however, be based on the history of Jesus or they will inevitably have a fragmentary, divided and therefore ideological relationship with reality. "Who has seen me has seen the Father" something of this must have been evident in history. (If there had been too great a division between these two levels, Christianity would never have stood any chance.) What is ultimately at stake is an affirmation which is made in faith and which claims to give consent to reality, even though that claim may be a claim based on faith.

We may, however, give our consent, in the language of faith, to a reality, in other words, to something that is not postulated as such by me as a believer, but which urges me to give consent and makes that consent an act of faith. In that case, the reality in question, the historical event of Jesus of Nazareth, must provide the basis of what is said about Jesus in the language of faith and at the same time fill it.

Within the context of this question, there are therefore two points in the interpretation of Jesus today which come together in what is often expressed, wrongly, in the form of a dilemma. Is salvation contained in the historical appearance of Jesus, in his challenging message and in his good and critical words and way of life, in which he was faithful to death? Or is salvation contained in Jesus who was crucified and rose from the dead? The two points involved here are, firstly, is the expression of God essential to the identity of Jesus (the "God of Jesus") and, secondly, if the first question is answered affirmatively, what does it mean if the message and the praxis of Jesus' life resulted in failure, in other words, were rejected (the "Jesus of God")?

1. *The "God of Jesus"*

We should not approach the "God of Jesus" expressed in Jesus' life from the vantage-point of a previously existing idea of what God is, as though we knew better who God is than who Jesus is. The only way in which we can gain a perspective of the "God of Jesus" is by examining the message of Jesus and the praxis of his life. This God was also both the God of Israel and the creator of heaven and earth. Jesus' appearance cannot, in other words, be isolated from his past, which was Israel. Moreover, even though he remains the focal point as well as the norm and criterion of the whole "event of Christ", he cannot be isolated from his past, his present, during which he went round in Palestine doing good, acting with and reacting to his contemporaries, and his future, which was the community of the Church which developed from him.

One of the data of Jesus' life which has a most firmly established historical basis is his expression of God in and through his message of the coming kingdom of God. This can be found in the traditions of the four gospels.[2] The content of this message of the kingdom emerges clearly from the original parables, in so far as these can be accurately reconstructed through the early Christian actualizations. The praxis of the kingdom of God is expressed above all in *metanoia* or conversion in these original parables and this central message is also filled with the praxis of Jesus' life, which is itself a parable of the kingdom of God.

"Rule" was a central concept in the ancient world, like "power". We do not find these concepts attractive, but, in Jesus' preaching and above all in his cures and and his driving out of devils, the concept of "rule" is opposed, as the power of love and goodness, to the powers of evil both within man and outside him.

[2] Luke 6. 20; Matt. 5. 3; Luke 7. 28; Matt. 11. 11; Luke 10. 9; Matt. 10. 7; Luke 11. 20; Matt. 12. 28, etc. Mark 1. 15; 4. 11; 4. 26; 9. 1, 27; 10. 14; 12. 34; 14. 25, etc. Matt, 3. 2; 4. 17; 5. 19, 20; 19. 24; 21. 31; 21. 43; Luke 4. 43; 9. 2, 11, 60, 62; 14. 15; 16. 16; 17. 20; 19. 11; 22. 16, 18; John 3. 3, 5.

A respect for God's supremacy and therefore for his rule is an essential part of Jesus' appearance and his message and he interpreted God's supremacy as an unconditional desire for man's good. God's rule is, for Jesus, not a function of human salvation —he is the man who experiences joy in God himself. God's rule is God's state of being God and our recognition of the rule or kingdom of God brings about our salvation, our state of being human.

This emphasizes a form of "rule" which is not oppressive, but liberating: "You know that the rulers of the Gentiles lord it over them, and their great men exercise authority over them. It shall not be so among you" (Matt. 20. 25–26). For Jesus, man's cause was God's cause, just as God's cause was also man's cause. This is clearly expressed in the Letter to Titus: "the goodness and the loving kindness (the loving mindfulness of man) of God appeared" (Tit. 3. 4).

The God of Jesus is undoubtedly God. He is not a function of humanity or of human liberation, but he is essentially a God who cares for man, with the result that the whole of Jesus' life was a "celebration" of God's rule and at the same time an "orthopraxis", in other words, a praxis in accordance (*orthōs*) with the kingdom of God. There is therefore an inner connection between the "kingdom" or "rule" of God and "orthopraxis" as a human phenomenon or a consistent translation of God's love of all men to the level of the praxis of human life. In this praxis, Jesus himself recognized the signs of the coming of God's rule, the kingdom of God. In the praxis of Jesus' own life, then, there was a proleptical or anticipatory realization in practice, not simply in theory, of the new world known as the "kingdom of God" and therefore a realization also of the new praxis that has been sought of a humane, good and true life. In Jesus, eschatological hope (the approaching kingdom of God) is linked with a new praxis of *metanoia*, the aspect of which that "shocks" man being expressed in the parables. The message of the approaching kingdom of God—and Jesus' life itself is a striking parable of this—therefore means salvation from God in Jesus manifested in a new praxis of human life, the living example of which is again Jesus himself.

Jesus was conscious that he had been called to invite, from

God, the host, all the guests, among whom were explicitly included all those who had hitherto been excluded from all communication and fellowship at table, namely the "tax collectors and sinners" (Mark 2. 15–17). The lost sheep, the man who was isolated from the group, had to be sought (Luke 15. 1–8; 19. 20; Matt. 9. 36; 10. 6). Jesus' striking solidarity with sinners and his association with them in order to open communication between them and God can be regarded as an offer of salvation, the "Good News" from God (Mark 1. 15).

Against the background of the current apocalyptic ideas and the convictions of the Pharisees, Essenes, Zealots and other similar "remnant" communities and movements, it is not easy to situate Jesus' message and his praxis in a religious and historical context. This is precisely why both his message and the praxis of his life cannot be understood without recourse to his own special and original experience of God. The history of suffering and of the absence of salvation within which Jesus' life was led provides no reason or basis for the certainty of salvation which characterizes Jesus' preaching. The hope expressed in his proclamation of the coming salvation of the world of men in the kingdom of God is clearly based on an experience of contrast. On the one hand, he lived in a human history of suffering characterized by the absence of salvation, peace and justice and by the presence of painful slavery. On the other hand, Jesus had the special experience of God as the one who promotes good and refuses to recognize the power of evil. Jesus' conviction and proclamation of the kingdom of God which set men free here and now in history were fashioned by this religious experience of contrast. He experienced God as the one who gives the future to those to whom no future can, from the worldly point of view, be promised.

Man is thus given a hope that cannot be traced back to his history in the world or to his personal or his social and political experience, yet it is none the less a hope that has at the same time to be fulfilled in this world in terms of man's personal and social and political salvation. Jesus was made conscious of the possibility of this hope by the original nature of his experience of God and this experience had been made possible by what had gone before in the religious life of prophetic Judaism. In other words, the best of Israel's experience of God reached an original and personal climax in Jesus—Yahweh as the one who was to come and who for the time being refused to present his credentials ("I shall be who I shall be, Exod. 3. 14). Believing in such a God was placing one's trust in one who took his identity very seriously and at the same time refused to reveal it fully "in advance". Jesus therefore experienced God as the power of good and "anti-evil", in other words, as man's salvation in the history of human suffering. The "God of Jesus" is a God to whom "all things are possible" (Mark 10. 27) and, in his words and his actions, Jesus has called on us to believe in this God. If we deprive Jesus of his relationship with God in his life and preaching, we deny his historical identity and make him into an "unhistorical" being, a "non-Jesus", someone who was in any case not "Jesus of Nazareth".

2. The "Jesus of God"

The essence of Jesus' identity that emerges from a critical analysis of the four gospels is that he was not himself concerned with his own identity, but wanted to identify himself with God's cause as man's cause and with the salvation, the wholeness, of man as God's cause.

While Jesus was living in history, a history which was contingent and unfinished, the revelation of salvation in God was, for anyone who was able to experience it in Jesus, also unfinished and still in a process of development. "Christology" is essentially a statement, made in faith, about the totality of Jesus' life, which is therefore presupposed in the Christian experience of "disclosure". It is only Jesus' completed life which is God's revelation in Jesus of Nazareth. Our story of Jesus can only really begin with Jesus' death, as the closure of his whole life, even though our story of Jesus or our recognition of Christ must also be a recognition of Jesus of Nazareth and not a myth or gnosis.

In fact, Jesus' message and the praxis of his life were rejected, because of the purely historical failure of his life and work. For this reason, his message and the praxis of his life, however important they may have been, cannot be the last word or the basis of real hope for us. This problem is resolved in the gospels by reference to faith in the resurrection and, while avoiding a full analysis of the emergence of faith in the resurrection, we are bound to consider its significance within the framework of what we have already said.

It is clear from the "missionary sermons" in Acts (10. 34–43; 2. 22–36; 4. 26–27; 3. 12–26; 13. 16–41) that there was a connection between Jesus and the Spirit. In these sermons, Luke throws light for the Greeks on the meaning of "Christ" as the one who was anointed with the Spirit—for example, declaring that God was with him (Acts 2. 22; 3. 14; 10. 38). Paul said similarly that "Christ is God's" (1 Cor. 3. 23). Jesus, in other words, was God's "possession"—this is clear from the same texts in Acts, which speak of "thy Holy One", "thy holy servant", "his servant", "his Christ", "my Son", and so on (Acts 2. 27; 3. 14; 4. 27; 13. 35; 3. 13; 3. 26; 4. 30; 3. 18; 13. 33).

Jesus' rejection by men was counterbalanced by Jesus' belonging to God. In these missionary sermons, then, believing in the earthly Jesus meant recognizing him as God's eschatological prophet of and for Israel, the last messenger from God who was to proclaim the kingdom of God as very close and to bring it in his words and his actions. Believing in the risen Jesus, on the other hand, was recognizing him in his universal significance as the saviour of all mankind. These two aspects are, however, defined by Jesus' belonging to God on the one hand and by God's faithfulness to Jesus on the other.

The resurrection—God made Jesus rise again—therefore confirms Jesus' message and the praxis of his life. It also reveals that his person is indissolubly bound to God and to this message. In Jesus' death and resurrection, man's rejection of God's offer of salvation and the constant provision of that salvation in the risen Jesus encounter each other. The risen Jesus is God's overcoming of man's rejection of the provision of definitive salvation from God in Jesus. God goes so far as to break through man's rejection in the resurrection of Jesus, in whom he gives the future to anyone who has no future and who merits no future. He loved us "while we were yet sinners" (Rom. 5. 8). He shows himself in the risen Jesus to be the power of good and "anti-evil", unconditional goodness which refuses to recognize the power of evil and breaks through it. In his supreme need, in his suffering and crucifixion, Jesus gave up his personal secret, the mystery of his person, his inviolable bond with God, while the Father also gave up his personal secret with regard to Jesus, his constant acknowledgment of Jesus. In this way, the Father-Son relationship is revealed in the death and resurrection of Jesus and we are therefore bound to ask the question about the Trinity.

When he sent Jesus to Israel, God fulfilled the promise of the Old Covenant and affirmed this and his creation. When Israel rejected this offer of salvation in Jesus, God brought about a "new creation" in and through the resurrection of Jesus. In the rejected but risen Jesus of Nazareth, then, the Old Testament was fulfilled and the New Testament was begun. There is a clear continuity between our human history and this new creation on the basis of Jesus' resurrection. At the same time, however, on the basis of the rejection of Jesus as the one through whom the covenant and creation itself were fulfilled, there is also a discontinuity which is inwardly connected with the historical continuity. This link is made by God's new saving activity which transcends the historical failure of Jesus, who fulfilled the covenant and creation, but who was rejected and crucified, and installs the rejected Jesus in a position where he can carry out his function of bringing universal salvation. Within our human history, the integration of Jesus' rejection and crucifixion into his offer of salvation, which is the meaning of his whole life, is the historical index of this transcendence. God has, in other words, redeemed us in Jesus Christ (see 2 Cor. 5. 14–18).

Jesus' resurrection is God's confirmation of his message and the praxis of his life precisely because his "belonging to God" was confirmed by God in the resurrection. This at the same time implies that the content of the eschatological liberation which is expressed in the language of faith as "resurrection from the dead" has to be filled in the light of Jesus' historical appearance, that is, of his words and actions which are confirmed by the crucifixion and resurrection. The question as to whether salvation is found in Jesus of Nazareth or in the crucifixion and resurrection is therefore a false dilemma. This is because Jesus of Nazareth is confirmed by God in the crucifixion and resurrection, whereas this confirmed crucifixion and resurrection is filled concretely in Jesus of Nazareth. In other words, a crucified Jesus who rose from the dead remains a myth or a gnostic mystery without Jesus of Nazareth. In spite of the astonishing message and the praxis of Jesus' life, without the resurrection Jesus of Nazareth would have been a failure, like all the failures of innocent men in the history of human suffering. It would have resulted in a brief hope and would have confirmed the suspicion that many people do not accept it, but do experience its utopian character because of the very nature of their history.

There is therefore no rupture between "Jesus of Nazareth" and the crucified Jesus who rose from the dead. Jesus' death confronts us with a fairly fundamental question about God because of Jesus' life which preceded his death. One answer to this question is that God, whose kingdom Jesus proclaimed, was an illusion on the part of Jesus (and also a God in whom Jesus' disciples were disillusioned). A second possible answer is that Jesus' rejection and death compels us to revise our own understanding of God and even to abandon it as invalid, God's real nature appearing as valid only in Jesus' life and death. God, whom Jesus called absolutely reliable, is, in other words, either a tragic farce or else a God to whom we must confess in the preaching and in the historical failure of Jesus. Faith in Jesus can only occur in the form of a confession to God.

The rupture in this Christian faith is therefore not to be found in Jesus' death. He experienced that death as an involvement in his mission to offer salvation and as the historical consequence of his love and care for men. This is the minimum of essential historical truth that has to be preserved from the tradition of the Last Supper.) The break is rather to be found in the rejection of his message and the praxis of his life, which resulted in a rejection of his very person. God's confirmation in the resurrection therefore concerns the very person of Jesus and, in that person, his message and the praxis of his life. Both the rejection and God's confirmation of and consent to the person of Jesus therefore give validity to the specific aspect of the event of Jesus, in which the person of Jesus and his task in life (his message and his praxis) form an indissoluble unity. This is why the kingdom of God is able to have, in the Christian confession, the appearance of Jesus Christ and why we can speak about the "Lord Jesus Christ" as synonymous with the kingdom of God as proclaimed by Jesus.

In speaking about God's confirmation of Jesus' person, message and praxis, we have to bear in mind that this statement is also an affirmation of faith and not a confrontation or a legitimation in the purely human sense of the word. The resurrection confirms that God was always with Jesus throughout his whole life, even when he was humanly forsaken in his death on the cross, when God himself was silent. A conviction of faith, the resurrection, cannot be a legitimation of another conviction of faith, that of God's saving activity in Jesus of Nazareth. Any authentic legitimation, which is to be evident to all men, must therefore always be completely eschatological. This is why faith in the resurrection is a prophecy and a promise for this world and, as a prophecy, it is defenceless and vulnerable. Christian life is therefore not justified or made right by history. On the other hand, Christians, believing in the resurrection of Jesus, are liberated by their faith from the need to justify themselves and to claim that God has now to protect and ratify those who are faithful to him in public. The servant is, in other words, no better than the master. Like Jesus himself, the Christian dares to entrust himself to God and to trust that God will justify his life and he is ready to receive that justification, as Jesus did, beyond death. Because he has been reconciled to God's manner of acting in this way, he is also reconciled to himself, to others and to history, in which he none the less still tries to achieve emancipation and redemption. For this reason, he is able to be completely committed, without using violence, to make this world a more just and happy place for all men and to eliminate alienation. Like Jesus, however, the Christian cannot justify himself by producing his credentials, apart from his concrete praxis of the kingdom of God.

III. THE STORY OF JESUS: A PARABLE OF GOD AND A PARADIGM OF HUMANITY

The answer which enables Christians to recognize Jesus as the one who offers definite and definitive salvation from God and therefore to confess the "story of God" in the human story of Jesus cannot be distilled by an exegetical process from a deep analysis of New Testament texts, however necessary this may be if we are to know the real story of Jesus. This is because the mediated nearness of God's offer of mercy to man is conveyed in a more concentrated form than elsewhere in the revealing and the concealing mediation of Jesus. Nowhere else has there ever been such a concentration of concealing mediation—Jesus was even sent to his death in the name of orthodox religion. Nowhere else too is God's direct and gratuitous nearness in him so tangibly present for the one who, in *metanoia* (self-criticism), goes forward openly to meet him—in the tradition of the Church, he is even called the "true God". A person cannot be approached precisely as a person in a process of purely theoretical, scientific analysis. The one who is prepared to take a risk, however, can still recognize, in the story of Jesus, the great parable of God himself and at the same time the paradigm of our humanity, a new and unheard of possibility of existence offered because God himself was concerned with humanity. Part of the plot of the story of Jesus, however, is that his shocking freedom is a scandal to the one who takes offence at him (Luke 7. 23) and is at the same time able to act as a liberation to salvation in the case of the one who dares to trust the fascinating mystery of that story.

The question therefore arises as to whether too precise a theoretical definition of who Jesus Christ is is not more harmful than beneficial. A precise theoretical definition of a divine event which overwhelmed Jesus and which constitutes the heart and soul of his entire life empoverishes that event and is therefore likely to be near to distortion, one-sidedness and heresy. This is all the more likely in this case, since Jesus' death was violent. On the basis of a critically justified exegesis, it is essential to affirm Jesus' integration of his violent death into his surrender of himself to God and his offer of salvation to men. Despite this, however, it is impossible to deny the negativity of that death, as a rejection.

It is impossible, theoretically or rationally, to reconcile or mediate salvation on the one hand and the history of suffering on the other, especially when the latter is a history of the suffering of an innocent and just man.[3] On the one hand, salvation history took place in Jesus' life. This is a fact which cannot be eliminated by his death or suspended by it. On the other hand, however,

[3] E. Schillebeeckx, "Naar een definitieve toekomst: belofte en menselijke bemiddeling", *Toekomst van de religie. Religie van de toekomst* (Bruges and Utrecht, 1972), pp. 37–55, especially pp. 48–51.

Jesus' suffering and death, as a rejection, are, from the historical point of view, a pure absence of salvation. This negative aspect cannot be denied. It is impossible to achieve a theoretical, in other words, a rationally diaphonous reconciliation between these two aspects. For this reason, we are bound to conclude, with J. B. Metz, that salvation from God can only be expressed in the "non-identity" of the history of Jesus' suffering and death.[4]

This situates Jesus' suffering outside God and within the secular framework of the human predicament and human freedom and this suggests that Jesus continued to identify himself with God's cause without contaminating God himself by his own suffering precisely within this non-divine situation of suffering and death. Even with regard to Jesus, God remained free: "My thoughts are not your thoughts, neither are your ways my ways" (Isa. 55. 8). God's sovereign freedom applies to all men, but Jesus identified himself with this incomprehensible freedom of God in complete self-surrender at the approach of death. It was precisely in the non-divine aspect of his innocent suffering and death and therefore in the ultimately non-diaphanous aspect that Jesus persisted in his personal identification with the kingdom of God that was to come. God's sublime and definitive revelation thus occurred in his silent but extremely intimate nearness to the suffering and dying Jesus, who experienced, in his suffering and death, the depths of the human predicament and at the same time his inseparable belonging to God. This is what cannot be theoretically included within a rational system—it can only be the object of a testimony of faith.

We are therefore bound to be more careful in any attempt to define the soteriological significance of Jesus' suffering and death theoretically, above all because we are confronted here with salvation that cannot be expressed but does offer a basis for living. Our reluctance to do this also has repercussions on any attempt that we may make to define Jesus' personal identity theoretically. It is clear that Jesus is entirely both on God's and on man's side. His solidarity both with God in his sovereign freedom and with man is certainly the real definition of the kingdom of God who

[4] J. B. Metz, "Erlösung und Emanzipation", *Stimmen der Zeit*, 191 (1973), pp. 171–84.

is concerned with man and of that kingdom which was experienced by Jesus himself in the alienation of his innocent, non-divine suffering and death.

This means that the cross is not what J. Moltmann has called an "event between God and God", but rather the index of the anti-divine in human history, which is transcended from within in Jesus, through his belonging to God. This belonging to God in an anti-divine situation has brought us salvation. Jesus rejected all competition between God's honour and sublimity on the one hand and man's happiness and salvation on the other. But how can all this be given a more precise theoretical definition if it is impossible for us to define God himself more precisely and to define the meaning of humanity?

My intention is not to impose silence or to check reflection about this question. What I have in mind is that a mystery of love and solidarity such as this ought to be approached with a certain reverence. What is more, any "theoretical" theology should also be connected[5] both with "stories"[6] and, even more importantly, with orthopraxis. This orthopraxis is the praxis of the kingdom of God, without which any theory or story will cease to be credible, especially in a world which is demanding justice and freedom. When this is done, theory, story and the praxis of the kingdom of God will become an effective invitation to answer in real freedom the question: "But who do you say that I am?" (Mark 8. 29; Matt. 16. 15; Luke 9. 20).

Translated by David Smith

[5] It is, after all, possible to begin telling a story too soon.
[6] See J. B. Metz, *op. cit.*, and "A Short Apology of Narrative", *Concilium*, May 1973 (American edn., Vol. 85).

PART II
DOCUMENTATION

Gerhard Adler

The Jesus People and the Churches

WE have decided to say something about the Jesus People in this issue, even though their high-point in the public eye is now a thing of the past. We are convinced that the Jesus people (who appeared on the North American West Coast around 1967) raised problems of continuing ecclesiastical and theological relevance even though, after considerable delay and after some initial holding back, this new experience of Jesus is now reflected in the Church and in theology. The essence of the matter has been discerned more clearly behind the picturesque externals.

The Jesus movement is not an organization and one can only guess at the number of those who legitimately think of themselves as belonging to it; there must be hundreds of thousands of them. What this will mean in terms of a permanent feature of the religious scenery, initially in the States and then throughout the world, remains to be seen. The movement isn't monolithic, for its sources and roots are not homogeneous. The Jesus movement arose for the most part outside the usual church framework. That is true especially of the surprising wave of conversion among hippies and radical students. Representatives of some churches (primarily the Baptists) have discerned fruits to come in the movement, and have made themselves its field of operation.

A distinction must be made between this religious outbreak in the youth subculture and the revival movements of Free Church origins which already have a tradition to look back to, even though these trends soon united with the new ferment among students and hippies. There are elements of the American Free Churches in all groups which can be observed today. Sometimes the spirituality of the Pentecostals plays the dominant role, whereas on other occasions intellectual aspects are more noticeable.

There are reasons for and against counting the pentecostal movement in the Catholic Church in the USA (this applies to the Episcopalian Church, and so on) as part of the Jesus movement. On the one hand it is not comparable sociologically with the religious awakening in the counter-culture, or with the traditional revival campaigns, but on the other hand this Catholic pentecostal movement does correspond to the widespread desire for a more lively spirituality and fulfils an emotional need.

Its polymorphous character prevents any uniform evaluation of the movement. In addition to hopeful revival and conversion experiences, one has to take into account neurotic demagogues who, with their promise of the immediate return of Christ, mix a deep-lying end-of-the-world mood with anti-Communism and crude biblical exegesis, and summon people to flight from the world and a rejection of society, and to a not unproblematic drop in efficiency.

The few leaders (a major problem) are concerned with the combination of the diverse origins and cultural preconditions of the movement. In addition to the Free Church and pentecostal traditions with a strong emphasis on a literal understanding of the Bible, glossolalia, spiritual healing and prophecy, there are phenomena of the hippy subculture. In "Christian Houses" the life of the communes has found some kind of extension, and monastic traces may be seen. Disillusionment with politics was a spur for many to look for a new means of identification, a replacement for their abandoned hope in the world. A consciousness of socio-political responsibility is not always lost, however, for individualism is not the unique basic attitude. "Expansion" of consciousness with drugs and an encounter with Asiatic religions was for many a preliminary stage to the experience of Christianity. Traces of this process are still visible.

Hence the Jesus movement understandably possesses neither a uniform theology nor a universally binding spirituality, and even the emotional element is variously pronounced according to milieu. But common to all (and this applies also to the pentecostal currents in the major churches) is the experience of God as a living, personal reality, and not as a cypher for common humanity. The Bible is the binding word of God, which is valid here and now, is taken seriously and in which there is nothing to demythologize. Apart from the pride in election of some extremists, openness and missionary witness dominate—an enthusiasm which cares about understanding and tolerance.

The message of the Jesus People is simply that it is not enough to belong to a church if you want to be saved: Go to Jesus, who has already shed his blood for your sins. Acknowledge your sins, call him into your heart. Spiritual rebirth brings heaven into view but hell and its terrors are also pictured as realistically as earthly actuality. Here there is no theological precision, and a medieval dualism has hardly been surpassed. But despite all the anti-intellectualism and occasional excessive emotionality, we mustn't ignore the fact that the basic propositions of Christian belief are once again being taken seriously: the incarnation, cross, resurrection and expectation of the return of the Lord are at the centre of the emotionality of many Jesus People. It is unfortunate that there is no room for critical confrontation with the Bible, but one must try to understand that there is no need for that: for the most part these are genuine converts, who happily still experience the initial wonderment of the newly converted and try to experience to the full what they have gained. At the same time there is a lack of all prerequisite knowledge for intellectual disputation. Here the major churches must be very careful. The few leaders with any theological background have for the most part a fundamentalist understanding of the Bible—one which quite consciously distances itself from "liberal" theology.

Many ministers in the established churches are surprised, even envious, that in spite of all their efforts, the gospel suddenly found and continues to find such a considerable following outside the churches. Perhaps they should ponder a few questions: Was there sufficient room for emotional needs in the traditional services of the major churches? Aren't the parishes

far too middle-class, to such an extent that a youth of unconventional appearance must seem alien from the start in one of
the main-line churches? Have liturgical reforms and similar
efforts taken group-dynamic findings into account? Are the
spatially large churches with such small congregations really still
suitable for evoking a community feeling? But there are also
theological considerations: Hasn't the Christian message been
excessively rationalized, and adapted to the world so that the
specific content of the gospel has disappeared? Despite justifiable concern for the conditions prevailing in this world,
wasn't the dimension of the individual somewhat attenuated
—the dimension that young people have now rediscovered?
Then there is division among Christians—something quite incomprehensible to the Jesus People. The fact that historical
problems and theological difficulties are underestimated for the
most part does mean that there is not a real scandal here.
Whether the movement will develop as an ecumenical pressure
group, or (no less probable in view of American church history)
split into new denominations and sects, remains to be seen.

Buttons, posters and T-shirts with Jesus-movement symbols
have led to a special industry. One-way symbols, marantha
calendars and vulgar Christ images on underclothes seem dis-
tasteful to the European observer. But all that this shows is that
religion can be an object of business. Religion proper, spiritual
awakening, is not to be confused with the commercial, nor is
it identical with it. Commerce wouldn't be possible without
manifest profound religious feeling. Even in pop-music there
is a genuine religious element. And that brings us to the core
of the matter.

The Jesus movement, and not that alone, but many other
tendencies, offered by sectarian, syncretic or oriental forms of
religion, is essentially an attempt to make out a meaning of life
lying beyond materiality. Materialistic optimism is approaching
its end. Technology has solved technological problems, yet it
can't solve any human problems, but only makes new ones.
A mechanistically-oriented psychoanalysis is also useless as a
directive aid. The fact that the majority of the population has
reached a good standard of living has not enriched the human

quality of life. There has been a liberation from material needs, but no removal of loneliness, easing of the burden of old age, explanation of problems of death and after; and relations between man and wife, parents and children have not profited from this progress. The American nuclear family can to a considerable extent no longer view its function and tasks in the traditional sense. Technological and material progress has obscured that human area which now demands its rights.

Even the hippy movement was an attempt to break out of this diseased world which with increasing riches has become meaningless, and which with technological progress has increased new dangers and problems for itself which it hardly knows how to tackle. The American feeling of world dissolution (war in East Asia, the West European union, environmental pollution, economic recession, crime rates and the old race problem) is mixed with the old prophetic tradition of the USA Free Churches. Life anxiety increased by religious non-affiliation correlates on the US West Coast with a strong interest in oriental religions, meditation and mysticism, black magic, spiritualism and astrology. Even if the Jesus People are put into this framework they are not to be identified with it. Even the longing for biblical proclamation, for religious community, for signs and liturgy, prayer and penance in a social and psychological context, persists; or, expressed in the formula of Christian theology: *gratia supponit naturam.* The conviction of the Jesus People that the Holy Spirit is at work does not contradict that.

In all times of crisis in history and church history, groups and prophets arose who prophesied an imminent end to the world, or the return of Christ. The imminent expectation of the Jesus People belongs in this context. But here *marantha* is not a dogma. Whereas some expect the physical return of Christ, others have recourse to Jesus' words: "Wherever two or three are gathered together in my name, there I am in the midst of them" (Mt. 18. 20). Imminent expectation produces in many a not wholly innocuous, passive attitude to life. But that is not general. The objection that the movement is antipathetic to reality is unjust.

Where Jesus People have occurred outside the USA they have done so predominantly according to the American model.

Whether the mere translation of American patterns can be successful in the long run is doubtful. The taking over of a communications system without adaptation to local conditions should prove too inorganic to remain effective. That this religious experience on the American pattern has liberated people from drug-dependence (and many other burdens) in many other countries is no argument to the contrary. It has long been objected against young people by pessimists of the older generation, that they have no goal or ideals. If these young people (and there are many signs of this) are in search of the "lost dimension" when they change the content of their lives and try to work out the meaning of life, then at least one should be reluctant to judge them when everything isn't perfect, and when emotive and irrational aspects predominate. Materialism and technological rationality do not answer the question of meaning. If some young people are seriously turning to the gospel, that is a good starting-point, even though everything at first doesn't seem so very "rational" or "orthodox" as one would wish. In all justifiable criticism, in all warnings of evasion, unhistorical thinking and non-politcal commitment, the main thing shouldn't be overlooked: hundreds of thousands hear of the good news, hundreds of thousands who aren't reached by the Church.

The Church must concern itself with the integration of the Jesus People. But it shouldn't make the surrender of special features of the youth subculture a prerequisite for Christian community. The Jesus movement shows so many genuine Christian traces that it would be wrong to declare it wholly inadequate. It will be asked whether the Jesus freaks did not know something hidden from the wise and clever (Mt. 11. 25).

Translated by Verdant Green

Gustavo Gutiérrez-Merino

Liberation Movements and Theology

SEVERAL factors have caused man's political consciousness to mature at a swifter pace in recent years. These include various political happenings which have had a profound effect on history, the rapid development of science and consequent mastery of nature, the use of new instruments for the understanding of social reality and finally the cultural changes produced by all these phenomena. The social praxis of contemporary man has come to adult status. He now has a clearer picture of the way his life in society is conditioned, but he is also more conscious of being an active participator in history.

This political consciousness is sharpened when the contradiction grows between an increasing aspiration to secure effective freedom and justice, and the existence of a social order which claims to recognize freedom and justice in law, but in reality denies them in countless ways to social classes, entire peoples and racial minorities. Hence the revolutionary, militant search for the right conditions for the construction of a free, just society, and the attitude of critical suspicion towards any ideological argument designed to conceal a situation of cruelty and discord.

In the context of this new political consciousness the debate is being renewed in theological circles about the connection between Christian faith and political action. The subject is old but always fresh. It first arose when the gospel was preached to man and it still applies to man today. It has been treated differently at different stages of the historical development of the Christian community. Lines of thought advanced in the past form the heritage of ideas that is today being subjected to critical reassessment. Like any problem that is complex and full of implications, it is constantly changing focus through breaks with the past and the opening-up of new fields of investigation. We have reached an important milestone in the scrutiny of the relationship between the gospel message and the political world. This critical reassessment is polemical because it questions positions which were regarded as fixed, and because it impinges more and more aggressively on the social practice of Christians.

I. THEOLOGY AND POLITICS

The new political theology that orginated in Germany followed this line.[1] It did not propose the creation of a new theological discipline.[2] It took up a profoundly critical position rooted in the views of the Enlightenment on the political field as the arena of freedom. Hence the talk of a *new* political theology in opposition to previous approaches to theology which are defenceless in the face of the criticism of religion mounted by the Enlightenment (and by Marxism) and take refuge in a faith lived in the private sector. The opposition to this private view of faith, a necessary task, allows scope for criticism of the very fundamentals of our present-day theology[3] and for a reconsideration of the question of the way faith impinges on the on-going movement of history. Metz placed his finger on what is really at stake in the theology of today when he claimed that the so-called fundamental hermeneutical problem of theology was not really that of the relationship between systematic and historical theology or between dogma and history, but the relationship between theory and practice, between understanding faith and social practice.[4] The polemics surrounding political theology led it to define and clarify its positions. Besides, although conditioned by the political and cultural medium in

[1] Cf. J. B. Metz, *Theology of the World* (London, 1969). This work collects together writings between 1962 and 1967. See also *Idem*, "Politische Theologie in der Diskussion" in *Diskussion zur Politischen Theologie* (Mainz and Munich, 1970), and M. Xhaufflaire, La *"Théologie Politique"* (Paris, 1972).
[2] J. B. Metz, *op. cit.* pp. 106–7 in the German original.
[3] *Ibid.*, p. 101.   [4] *Ibid.*, p. 104.

which it arose, it was receptive to new currents of thought due
to pressures originating in other disciplines. This openness to
inquiry was possible because political theology goes straight to
the heart of questions which are basic to theology and urgent
for man and for the believer today.

Two movements of lesser scope but emphasizing some elements
not dealt with, initially at least, by political theology are encountered in what was called "the theology of development"
and the "theology of revolution".

After the Bandung Conference in 1955 the term development
began to express in a synthetic form the aspirations of men of
today for more human conditions of life. It was the miserable
situation of the so-called underdeveloped countries which threw
the problem into sharp relief. Papal encyclicals and Vatican II
recognized the problem and theological thought began to crystal-
lize on this subject.[5] Theology sought to evaluate the effort to
transform nature and to create a more just and more human world.
Biblical texts on work were appealed to, and there was talk of
the vocation of the Christian to control the earth and make it
more habitable for man. The overall view was optimistic and
dynamic. Human progress was seen as a biblical requirement
and a condition for a fuller life of faith. There was, however,
too much dependence on the concept of development and especially on its implicit political context. Nor was sufficient account
taken of the true causes of the misery and injustice in which
poor nations live, or of the strife-ridden character of human
history.[6] Certain texts of *Populorum Progressio* signified, from
the theological point of view, an important step forward for
this line of thought, because they clearly put the efforts to build
a better society in the context of the total salvation of Christ.[7]
This intimate relationship, which the encyclical embraced with
the term integral development, was later taken up by other

---

[5] Cf. the bibliography prepared by G. Bauer and published by Sodepax,
Towards a Theology of Development, Annotated Bibliography (Geneva,
1970).

[6] See a criticism of this view in G. Gutiérrez, *Teología de la Liberación.
Perspectivas* (Lima, 1971; Madrid, 1972).

[7] Cf. R. Laurentin, *Développement et Salut* (Paris, 1969), which takes
this viewpoint into account.

schools of thought, again using biblical terms and sources to clarify it.

The theology of revolution was initially elaborated by theologians who had a first-hand knowledge of countries experiencing the revolutionary process. A certain German theology became a sounding-board for the theology of revolution, taken out of its own context, and it was subsequently translated in Latin America[8] The fundamental note of this view is that "decisions on the great questions facing civilization will have to be made in a context of revolution in the world today by those who are responsible for the well-being and the future of man".[9] An attempt was made to see the Christian faith in the light of this challenge. Revolutionary commitment was depicted as radically questioning the established social order and political analysis began to take account of the fact of the confrontation between social classes. Faith appeared as motivating and justifying Christian participation in the revolutionary process. When the gospel was stripped of any ideological element which falsified a cruel, divided social reality, it was seen as not opposed to the revolution, but as demanding it. Although this theology had the merit of trying to destroy the image of a faith bound to an unjust social order, it ran the risk of becoming a "revolutionary Christian ideology". Well received by some Christians who were taking their first steps towards participating in the revolutionary process, this theology soon revealed its limitations when the attempt was made, sometimes despite itself and its initiators, to "baptize" the revolution. Its theological failings became evident when it was put forward simply as an *ad hoc* statement of revolutionary principles, with a rather fundamentalist approach to some Old Testament texts in particular.

What is more—and this is important for our purpose—the starting-point and therefore the way of thinking of the theology

[8] Cf. the works collected by E. Feil and R. Weth, *Diskussion zur Theologie der Revolution* (Mainz and Munich, 1969).

[9] R. Shaull, "Point de vue théologique sur la Révolution", in *L'Ethique sociale chrétienne dans un monde en transformation* (Geneva, 1966), p. 14. This author may be regarded as the initiator and best representative of the theology of revolution; his intuitions go beyond anything subsequently written on this subject. For a broad view, see also J. Comblin, *Théologie de la Révolution* (Paris, 1970).

of development and of the theology of revolution showed no change. Efforts to further development or revolutionary action were regarded as the *application* of a certain process of theological thought to certain aspects of the political world this time, but there was no question of a new kind of apprehension of faith. It was not theological thought in the context of the process of liberation. It was not critical thought from and about the historical praxis of liberation, from and about faith as a liberating praxis. To theologize from this later standpoint certainly involves a change of perspective.

II. Theology in the Context of Liberation

Man today is filled with the desire for liberation. The exercise of genuine freedom appears more and more clearly as an historical achievement, as the result of a process. The liberating process frees man from everything that limits or impedes him from fulfilling himself. This desire for liberation is experienced above all by the exploited social classes of the poor countries which are struggling to free themselves from the classes that oppress them, by racial minorities that are discriminated against and by oppressed cultures. This fact does not restrict matters to the merely political field—on the contrary, it focuses attention on all the dimensions of man which are involved in the process of liberation.

Theologians today are engaged in a discourse on faith which takes as its starting-point the praxis of liberation, from a position of real and effective solidarity with the poor, the marginal race, the victimized classes. This kind of reflection could only occur when the participation by Christians in the praxis of liberation had reached a certain stage of maturity and depth. This is what has been called the "theology of liberation".[10] It arises in Latin America within the Christian communities which are committed to the process of liberation.[11] It does not originate in a desire to

[10] Some bibliographies on this theme give the impression of an abundant literature, but this is deceptive, because different themes are included, there are many repetitions and works of doubtful value are mentioned.
[11] Cf. G. Gutiérrez, *Hacia una teología de la liberación* (Montevideo, 1969), which is the text of a lecture given in July 1968; see also *idem*,

justify this commitment, but is the fruit of a faith lived and considered amid the challenges aroused by the praxis of liberation and trying to make participation in the praxis more creative and critical. This kind of relationship defines its approach and enables it to re-read theological views of the past and select critically anything these have to contribute. It also means that the views of the theology of liberation operate from a different starting-point.

1. *A different cultural world*

For a Christian participation in the praxis of liberation is an opportunity to come into contact with a kind of reasoning different from that commonly employed in theology. It is also an opportunity for a demanding, fertile spiritual experience. Both of these factors are the result of entry into a different world, the world of the other man, that of the poor, the oppressed, the exploited classes. The identification of oneself with the interests and struggles of this "other man" of a social order built up in its economic, political and ideological aspects by a few men for their own benefit, is the central idea on which hinges a whole new way of being a man and living the Christian faith.[12] This rationale takes as its immediate context the radical challenge to an oppressing society and, closely related to this, the construction of a social order which is qualitatively different. In this new

---

"Notes on Theology of Liberation", a contribution to a conference organized by Sodepax in 1969 and published in *In search of a theology of development* (Lausanne, 1970); E. Pironio, *La Iglesia pueblo de Dios* (Bogota, 1970); *idem, La Iglesia que nace entre nosotros* (Bogotá, 1970); H. Assmann, *Opresión-liberación, desafío a los cristianos* (Montevideo, 1971); J. C. Scannone, "La teología de la liberación", in *Revista del centro de investigación y acción social*, 221 (Buenos Aires, April 1973), pp. 5-10; L. Gera, "Teología de la liberación", in *Perspectivas de diálogo* 72 (Montevideo, May 1973), pp. 38-49. Beyond all doubt, however, it was the texts of the Episcopal Conference of Medellín of 1968 which brought to public attention the theme of liberation as the pivot for apprehending faith. To this there must be added works written from different perspectives, cf. J. H. Cone, *A Black Theology of Liberation* (Philadelphia and New York, 1970); R. Ruether, *The Radical Kingdom* (New York, 1970), who has other works in course of preparation.
    [12] Cf. G. Gutiérrez, "Evangelio y praxis de liberación", in *Fé cristiana y cambio social* (Madrid, 1973), pp. 231-45; E. Dussel, *Para una ética de la liberación latinoamericana*, II (Buenos Aires, 1973).

order, social appropriation of the means of production would be accompanied by social appropriation of the conduct of politics and, finally, of liberty; so preparing the way for a new social consciousness. If this aim appears romantic and emotional to some of our contemporaries, it is because they do not appreciate the human values present in this challenge. As a consequence, the historical project and its underlying rationale is alien to them, i.e. the forging of a society geared to the poor and the dispossessed, and the making of a new man, no longer a slave but the agent of his own destiny. This rationale is orientated towards the transformation of history, and therefore begins from a different way of knowing and relating to historical practice. Like any achievement of human thought, the process that has led to this is long, but in our days it has reached a maturity which alters man's way of learning about himself. With the birth of experimental science, man is playing a more active role in acquiring knowledge. He no longer limits himself to contemplating nature and classifying what he observes. Instead, he interrogates and provokes it, discovers its laws and dominates it by technique. When the social and psychological sciences appeared, this kind of knowledge extended to fields of thought which until then were the preserve of philosophy. With the opening up of new paths of inquiry, philosophical reflection keeps all its importance and significance in a process of mutual enrichment with the human sciences.

All this has revealed something which stands as a basic feature of modern consciousness; namely that knowledge is linked to transformation. History is known only by transforming it and transforming oneself. Truth for the man of today is verified in the full etymological sense of the word—it is *made*. A knowledge of reality which does not lead to a modification of it is an interpretation which is not verified, not *made truth*. Historical reality ceases to be the field of application of abstract truths and idealist interpretations, and becomes the privileged place from which we start and to which we return in the process of knowing. The transforming historical praxis is not the action resulting from the incarnation at a lower level, of an assured, well-thought-out theory. It is rather the matrix of genuine knowledge and the proof of its value.

The liberating praxis also leads to a rich, demanding spiritual experience.[13] Thanks to it we can perceive elements of our encounter with the Lord in the encounter with our neighbour, the poor man of the gospel, who is left out of other approaches. A spiritual experience means a way of living in the Spirit our situation of sons of the Father and brothers of men.[14] The creation of brotherhood among men today is by way of solidarity with the poor and the exploited. From that solidarity we become brothers of all men and so receive the free gift of sonship. All this presupposes a real process of conversion, the keystone of all spirituality. Conversion according to the gospel means a radical transformation of ourselves, it means to think, feel and live like Christ present in the dispossessed and alienated. It follows that this is not a private, inward-looking attitude, but a process conditioned by the cultural, political and socio-economic medium in which we live and which must be transformed. Conversion takes man in all his dimensions, and implies a break with our mental categories, with our cultural background and our social class. Conversion always means going out of oneself and openness to the Lord and to others. This is what it is all about, life in the presence of the Lord at the heart of political activity with a full realization of all this entails in terms of conflict and of the demand for a scientific rationale.

2. A discourse on faith

Without these elements of a new spiritual thought and experience there can be no real discourse about faith. Theology is merely the awareness, in the community of the Church, which Christians experience of faith at a given moment in history. At the roots of any understanding of faith there is an experience of the Lord—a genuine theology is always a spiritual theology. But discourse on faith stands just as much in need of the tools of reasoning. Both aspects are present, at least initially, in a re-

[13] Cf. recent texts of Latin American Christian communities in *Signos de liberación* (Lima, 1973). Consult on this question the study of R. Muñóz, *Nueva conciencia de la Iglesia en América Latina* (Santiago de Chile, 1973). (To be published in Madrid by Ediciones Sígueme.)
[14] Cf. A. Paoli, *Diálogo de liberación* (Buenos Aires, 1970).

reading of the gospel from the standpoint of the praxis of liberation.

The word of the Lord received in faith will be lived and thought out today by a man who moves within certain cultural categories, as it was in the past by men formed by Greek thought. In these categories there is a new relationship between knowledge and transformation, theory and practice. This requires a re-reading of the gospel, which leads us to rediscover something perhaps forgotten or at least neglected in its implications by scriptural hermeneutics, viz. that the gospel truth is something which we have to work at.

John tells us to be doers of the word, which is truth, and this truth is love. To live love is to proclaim God. This does not mean a mechanical correspondence with the modern insistence on linking knowledge with transformation and on living a truth which is being verified. But the cultural world in which we live offers a starting-point and shows the way ahead for the advance of theological thought along a new road, yet with continued and necessary reference to its own sources. In this complex task we have to use numerous special skills in order to acquire a thorough knowledge of different aspects of contemporary thought. We must have recourse not only to a philosophy in dialogue with the human sciences, but also to the instruments offered by these, if we are to get to know the social realities which obstruct the social justice and brotherhood we seek. It is only in this way that action will become effective.

To carry out theological work in the ambit of a system of reasoning which incorporates elements distinct from those which traditional theology is accustomed to handle, creates conflicts and misunderstandings. This was always the case—in the past, general hostility and accusations of distorting and "humanizing" the faith opposed the use of Aristotelian philosophy in theology.[15] In the present instance, the task proposed—like others in the past—is on a more modest scale, but the virulence of some reactions is no less extreme. They can, perhaps, be accounted for by reasons not wholly theological. They form a part

[15] Cf. J. L. Segundo, "Desarrollo y subdesarrollo: polos teológicos" in *Persp. de dial.* 43 (May, 1970), pp. 76–80.

of the defence of a social order which is not disposed to be challenged and swept away by the man whom it despoils and keeps on the margin.

Seen in this light, theology is thinking critically from and about the historical praxis confronted with the Word of the Lord lived and accepted in a faith which reaches us through numerous and at times ambiguous historical mediations, but which we keep on working at day after day. Theology is thinking from the standpoint of the faith about faith as the praxis of liberation. It is an understanding of faith conducted from a commitment to solidarity with the oppressed classes and starting from their world. It is thought inspired by hope in God who reveals himself and reveals to man the fullness to which he is called. It is a theological discourse which makes itself true, in its real, fertile participation in the process of liberation.

In the attempt to think the faith from this cultural world, liberation appears as one single process, though its unity is in fact complex. Liberation gathers and knits together all the implications of the political struggle for a more just society and at the same time it takes on the character of historical conquest involved in the genuine exercise of human liberty, and binds them to the saving work of Christ.

This saving action goes straight to the roots of all social injustice and all absence of human brotherhood which is what sin is, a break in friendship with God and among men. It gives a gratuitous, unexpected fullness to human efforts for liberation. The growth of the kingdom of God occurs historically in political liberation, in so far as this allows man to realize himself more fully. But it goes beyond this. The kingdom of God condemns from within historical instances of liberation, their limitations and ambiguities, proclaims their complete fulfilment and impels them effectively towards total communion. There is no question here of disembodied simpliste misrepresentations, spiritualism or politico-religious messianism. Without liberating historical events there is no growth of the kingdom, but the process of liberation will not overcome the root causes of oppression and of man's exploitation by man, until the coming of the kingdom, which is, above all, a gift of the Lord.

These implications are and always will be a difficult and at the same time fertile field for theology. It has to find the precise terms in which to express them, and will have to avoid the danger of inadequate, impoverished definitions; but above all, it must interpret an experience of faith in the God who is revealed in history, acts in history and becomes man. In Christ, man gives God a human face, and God gives man a divine face.[16] The challenge facing the theology of liberation is to preserve all the riches of this unity, without falling into confusion: it is the challenge facing all theology.

The theology of liberation is a theology of salvation in the concrete historical and political conditions of today. These historical and political mediations of the present, evaluated at their true consistency, change our way of living and thinking about the love of the Father, human brotherhood and salvation. This is what the term liberation stands for.

III. PERSPECTIVES

The theology of liberation poses fundamental questions in the field of theological methodology. It above all draws attention to the importance for theological discourse of a theory of knowledge and a rationale linked to the project of a society constructed in the service of the poor and the exploited classes. But this is only the starting-point for a deeper, more exact understanding of what is involved. If this does not take place we will find, as indeed we do find today, that the expression "theology of liberation" and its derivatives, are being used to dress up old theological and pastoral attitudes with "social concern" and fashionable phraseology.

If, as we have seen, the experience of participation in the praxis of liberation is fundamental for this theological perspective, greater communication will be necessary among the various efforts that are being conducted in different contexts by men committed to a revolutionary programme. There have still been few attempts at contact among the theological positions that have been established in the committed Christian

[16] Cf. L. Boff, *Jesucristo libertador* (Petrópolis, 1972).

communities of Africa, Asia, in the racial minorities of the developed countries, and in Latin America. The rudimentary theology of liberation which we possess today would gain much from this encounter.[17]

Faith reaches us through historical mediations. The task of theology involves a critical examination of the forms in which the living of the faith in the political practice of Christians has been conveyed throughout history and is being conveyed today. If this is not done, we still remain at an abstract, non-historic level. We shall betray the fundamental intuition from which the theology of liberation springs, and fall into new ideological uses of Christianity. This latter factor will not be avoided merely by employing the term "liberation". Although this theological approach began from the problem of the significance of faith in its relation with the world of politics, the positions taken up have gradually led to a treatment of the great, classical questions of theology. The re-reading of the gospel from the praxis of liberation does not stop at this initial problem as if it were a chapter of theology apart. The central theme of salvation is looked at again from a new standpoint, and this opens up new vistas for the scrutiny of the classical questions of theology.

All this is important, but must not make us forget that the exegesis of a line of theological thought is carried out on events. Theological discourse carries out a mediating function between one manner of living the faith, and the communication of faith. While theology is a re-reading of the gospel, this is done with the purpose of proclaiming the message to men. The value and true worth of a specific way of apprehending faith is what is at stake here and this will be judged by the impact on human history of the gospel message to the poor and of the liberation message to the oppressed of our time.

Translated by J. P. Donnelly

---

[17] Cf. also the works of G. Girardi, *Cristianesimo, liberazione umana, lotta di classe* (Assisi, 1972); J. Alfaro, *Esperanza cristiana y liberación del hombre* (Barcelona, 1972); B. Olivier, *Développement ou libération* (Paris, 1973).

Juan Carlos Scannone

The Theology of Liberation—Evangelic or Ideological?

ONE of the key words of our time is "liberation", because it sums up much of what men of today aspire after, particularly in the Third World. The liberation movements of the Third World have made this word the theme of their discussions and it has been accepted into the language at all levels, including that of theology. The significant fact that looms larger with every passing day is that many Christians, many theologians and even the churches themselves in their official documents are committing themselves to the liberation of men and of peoples.

Theology, reflecting critically about the praxis of the Church and the whole historical praxis in the light of the word of God, *interprets and appropriates* this process of liberation which is now at work in society. This explains why the theology of liberation is taking shape in a more or less carefully thought-out fashion all over the world.

Its rise has provoked strong and opposing feelings. This is a sure sign that theological discussion has touched a sensitive point, a sign of the times, in which the believer can see the presence of the Lord. This fact alone constitutes an appeal for the use of discernment, a factor all the more necessary today, when we are bound to ask to what extent in the theology of liberation are the gospel and ideology intermingled. This question is asked by defenders of the *status quo,* but it is *immanent* within the theology of liberation itself.

The reflections which follow will centre, for obvious reasons, on the theology of liberation as it is being advanced in Latin

America. First I shall describe it briefly and distinguish it from the theology of revolution. Then I shall demonstrate its evangelical meaning and thirdly I shall indicate how it must necessarily be confronted with the question of its relationship with the ideologies of liberation. Finally I shall deal with the question of discernment already mentioned.

I. The Theology of Liberation—A Brief Description

Latin America is at the same time a part of the Third World and a continent which for the most part is Christian. This situation has meant that the realization of its state of structural dependence has had repercussions on the praxis and the understanding of faith. It has also meant that the recognition that the fight for justice and a sharing in the transformation of the world is a constituent dimension of the preaching of the gospel, and has acquired a specific meaning among us: that of an urgent, all-embracing and radical (in other words, revolutionary) change in the structures of injustice and dependence.

The theology of liberation is the interpretation and critical consideration of this process in the light of faith. The Christian faith undergoes a new experience: beginning from the Bible, it gets down to the task of transforming the world in a situation of dependence, and beginning from the praxis it goes back and re-reads the Bible. The theology of liberation is simply the theological momentum set up by this new experience. It is not just a chapter in theology, as the theology of development might be, or the theology of any earthly reality to which theological methodology might normally be applied. This is a new way of looking at the task of theology, which nevertheless retains something of its traditional elements. It not only reflects in the light of the Word *about* the praxis of liberation, but *from within* this praxis reinterprets the riches of faith, which itself is a praxis.

This theology is not the fruit of the academic work of isolated theologians. When we spoke of the praxis of liberation and of the faith as praxis, we referred to the praxis of the people of God, not only to that of the theologian, who is merely the reflecting, critical interpreter of the people.

II. The Theology of Liberation and the Theology of Revolution

Both in Europe and in Latin America there are people who confuse these two theologies. The theologians of liberation[1] make the following objections to the theology of revolution. Firstly, its viewpoint impoverishes the whole theological and political problem by isolating the subject from its overall theological context and the necessary socio-analytical processes. Secondly, it runs the risk of "baptizing" the revolution by providing an *ad hoc* Christian ideology and disregarding the level of political analysis of such commitments. Thirdly, there is the danger of affirming a direct and immediate relationship between faith and politics, which could result in claiming to deduce, on the basis of theological categories, what the revolution must do, what kind of revolution it must be and how it should be carried out strategically. As can be seen, these criticisms are not based on circumstantial detail but arise from the understanding that is held of the relationship between faith and politics.

III. The Evangelical Meaning of the Theology of Liberation

The wide-ranging scope of the theology of liberation shows its evangelic inspiration, which will be confirmed when its approach to its central theme is expounded. This theme is salvation, understood in its full integrity.

The people's call for liberation is a sign of the times. For the ears of faith it is *one* word of God which is interpreted in the light of *the* word of God. It becomes the starting-point for the praxis of liberation as charity in active operation, and also for the theological thinking which corresponds to it and in so doing is the theology of liberation.

From within the faith, this call makes itself heard through the analysis of poverty compiled by the social sciences. The theology of liberation therefore views the poor not only on an

[1] Cf. G. Gutiérrez, *Teología de la liberación, Perspectivas* (Madrid, 1972), p. 316; H. Assmann, *Opresión-liberación. Desafío a los cristianos* (Montevideo, 1971), pp. 107–14.

individual I-Thou level, but also structurally, as peoples oppressed and classes exploited by a system of domination. Taking an integral theological view, it will recognize in this situation a "sinful" situation, and emphasize that the root of all oppression is sin in the heart of man, of social classes and of whole peoples.

This understanding of the conflict between grace and sin and consequently of the Easter mystery leads to a preference for subjects such as those of the exodus and the new man. The liberation of Israel included political liberation but was not restricted to that, and the new man recreated in Christ's image is not only interior; he is also total and social.

The theology of liberation tries to overcome problems of dualism by taking seriously man's unique vocation to salvation. It exposes the ideological untruth of separating the love of God from the love of man, person from people, historical liberation from eschatological salvation. It overrules any static distinction on the basis of planes, and instead, distinguishes dimensions of the same concrete reality, in the eschatological tension, "now but not yet", within one history. Historical, political, social, etc., liberations are now saving achievements but are also a foretaste, a sign, an anticipation of the total, definitive liberation which is not yet consummated.

IV. ONE HISTORY

We are aware that the theme of one history, that is the unifying relationship between profane history and the history of salvation, has not yet been thoroughly worked out from the new viewpoint. It is being given a great deal of consideration nowadays.

However, a danger present in one of the currents of the theology of liberation (represented, for example, by H. Assmann) derives perhaps from the Hegelian influence received through Marxism. This is the danger that the *kenōsis* of the specifically Christian content in one history is conceived in such a way that the Christian element is absorbed by the secular. That is why, for example, the central paragraphs of the final document of the conference "Christians for Socialism" see history primarily from a secular standpoint (that of the socio-historical sciences), and follow the lines of Marxist method in their understanding of the Latin-American process. Reality is seen not so much from the standpoint of faith common to all Christians, but in the first place from the standpoint common to the Latin-American revolutionary, even though the Christian sees it also from within his faith. The result is that it is not clear whether the revolutionary commitment which is the starting-point for thinking (and for rethinking the theological content) can itself be questioned from within the faith or only in its eventual, later deviations. The risk is that the revolutionary commitment will be given an absolute ideological value, and liberation and revolution will be understood in a univocal fashion.

On the other hand a different approach to the theology of liberation is reflected, for example, in the theological documents of the Movement of Priests for the Third World, inspired by L. Gera. In this, one history is seen primarily from the standpoint of the faith, common to all Christians, although the context for the understanding of the faith is a specific socio-analytical interpretation (not Marxist) of Latin-American dependence. There are two consequences of this different way of viewing the question. First, in the interaction between faith and the praxis of liberation, the understanding of liberation and revolution can be freed from within the faith, of any risk of being made absolute or univocal. Secondly, the commitment to liberation and revolution can also be freed from this risk.

V. Theology of Liberation and Ideologies of Liberation

The theology of liberation is keenly aware of the need to excise the ideological content of those theologies which have unwittingly adopted the ideology of the dominant culture. As we have mentioned, it also rejects a Christian ideology for revolution. It is nevertheless accused of conniving with secular ideologies of liberation, and of being the tool of Marxism or other revolutionary movements. The relationship of the theology of liberation to ideologies of liberation is a question that must be faced. Its rejection of all dualism emphasizes the historical incarnation and the practical, effective realization of revealed

Truth. It encounters the historical mediations of faith—the socio-analytical interpretations through which the faith reads the signs of the times, or the utopias which announce and anticipate the hope of the eschatological kingdom or the political mediations through which charity operates. In all these cases, theology encounters the ideologies as it thinks in faith about the praxis and from inside it.

The historical mediations referred to imply ethical-political commitments at the three levels mentioned. Firstly, there is the level of the rational, scientific analysis of reality, which always implies a commitment to the analytical method used (never neutral), and to an interpretation of the data analysed. Secondly, there is the level of commitment to an historical project, which is never totally deduced from the analysis but includes an ethical "plus" element derived from the human capacity to take history as the field for responsible action. Thirdly, there are the levels of concrete, practical implementation of the project, that is, those of strategy and tactics.

It is precisely in these commitments that the problem is encountered. To the extent that they are political rather than ethical, they involve a relation with ideologies, but to the extent that they are ethical rather than political options, they concern theology. Sin or salvation is at stake in them, not only because of their content but because they are ethical commitments, which existentially are either saving or sinful. It is the function of theology as far as possible to think about the discernment of the saving presence of God in the praxis of liberation.

VI. Towards a Reply—First Approaches

A tentative first reply to the problem is given by the distinction, so frequent in Latin America, between two concepts of ideology. However, the mere distinction between ideologies which legitimize the *status quo* and ideologies of liberation does not suffice, for the latter type are not always genuinely liberating in the evangelic sense. A rethinking of this distinction derives from the Latin-American re-evaluation of the ideologies. "Scientism" is criticized as the ideology (in a pejorative sense) of the modern age, which classical Marxism is not free from either.

Scientism gives little weight to the human, popular project, in which peoples put forward their ideals, values and aspirations for liberation. Such historical projects are sketchily elaborated and consist of a total rejection of the present social structure and the affirmation of the values which it tramples upon and also of actions which indicate symbolically the lines of development of the new society that is to be set up.

This is clearly not an ideology in the pejorative sense, legitimizing opposition to change or claiming a total reply to the question of history. Rather than ideology, utopia should be the term used. The utopias, according to Gustavo Gutiérrez, mediate between faith and politics.

Paul VI says of utopias that "they can meet anew the Christian summons if they reject no opening" (Oct. Adv. n. 37). Therefore, even in the case of utopias, discernment becomes indispensable. An ideology in the negative sense may lurk within them, shutting them off from one or other human dimension, from the changes of history or from transcendence. In historical projects, and in the ethical-political commitments which involve them, the voices of liberating grace and of sin are intermingled, that is to say, the theological imperative of liberation and the illusions derived from bastard interests.

A second tentative reply is a kind of *argumentum ad hominem*. The theologian cannot evade the confrontation with ideologies, since he begins to theologize from within a social situation conditioned by particular interests. Still more, he cannot theologize without positing (even unconsciously) some human social project. This is either because he criticizes the ethical-political commitment in which he spontaneously moves (a commitment made by others) and so initiates an opposing commitment by this very act or because he accepts it as obvious. If he happens to decide not to commit himself, his abstention involves an implicit resignation to the dominant historical project. He cannot escape from the concrete political stresses of the history within which he moves, because he is a man.

VII. Theology of Liberation and Discernment

The theologian cannot, as we said, evade the pressure of opposing commitments, but he is not trapped by it either, because he can transcend it by discernment. This transcendence, however, is not a flight to some aseptic plane of non-history, prehistory or supra-history, but a transcendence incarnate in history itself, which through grace has the structure of a sign and a sacrament. Within the commitments and beyond their representative content (ideological or utopian) the theological message is encountered which becomes incarnate in history but is irreducible to ideologies and utopias. These latter may mediate it, disfigure it and even reject it, but from within it, they themselves can be discerned and judged.

Neither the static dualism of a distinction of planes, nor the dialectical absorption of theological by mundane values, takes any account of the incarnation of eschatology in history, free from all confusion or division. This incarnation, like Christ's, is liberating. It frees mundane values in their autonomy and openness to God. It frees liberty itself, for the discernment of the historical presence of the salvation and for the creation of history. Yet it leaves God free in his transcendence. Where the Spirit of Christ is, there is freedom.

We remarked previously that in the theology of liberation the faith is mediated historically both in the upward path of interpretation of the Latin-American socio-political reality and in the downward path of its concrete expression in the liberating praxis within which thought operates. The discernment and consequent liberation noted in the preceding paragraph can and must be present in both of these movements,[2] from below as well as from above. Our view is that they are present in many contributions from this theology, although not always.

Operating from below on the interpretation of reality, theology takes such phenomena as the theory of dependence, articulates them in the language of faith and places them in an ambit of freedom. That is to say, it makes this kind of interpretation

[2] Cf. my work: "Teología y política. El actual desafío planteado al lenguaje teológico latinoamericano de liberación" in *Fe cristiana y cambio social en América Latina, Encuentro de El Escorial, 1972* (Salamanca, 1973), pp. 247-64.

relative by stripping it of any ideological claim to be total, absolute exclusive truth. It liberates such interpretation from a meaning restricted to the sphere of economics, politics or social matters, and redresses the imbalance of their univocal language, opening it to the unforeseeable quality of new situations. (The fact that this meaning is open does not prevent it from being determined by the situation it set out to analyse.) Operating from above towards the praxis, the theology of liberation frees utopia from the danger of being regarded as definitive and total. It is allowed to be what it is: a utopia, essentially open in the tension of "now but not yet". Political action and commitment are respected for their contingent, relative nature, and are not deprived of the efficacy conferred on them by the absoluteness of charity.

The theology of liberation does not always achieve its liberating purpose. This is not due to the structure of the theological method adopted, nor to the new global challenge of theology. It is due to the failure to exercise to a sufficient extent critical thought about the historical praxis in the light of faith. Faith criticizes ideologies in their aim to restrict, totalize, absolutize. This is equally applicable to conservative ideologies and revolutionary ones (Marxist-inclined, or national-populist). Faith also embraces the utopias, without being identified with them, in so far as they are subjected to saving discernment and open themselves to the fullness of human values, to historical innovation and to God. This discernment is effected not only in the praxis, but also through it.

The appropriation of utopia by theological thought at the triple levels of ethical-political commitment previously mentioned is a feature of the theology of liberation. If it is faithful to its method and perspective, to the extent that it is faithful to them it respects the autonomy of science in its interpretation of reality, that of peoples in its creation of liberating historical projects and that of political action in its descent to the field of strategy and tactics. In this way it never fails to respect the transcendence of faith as the final key to the interpretation of reality, the transcendence of hope, open to the eschatological kingdom, and that of charity as transforming concrete, specific action.

One qualification must be made here. The theology of liberation provides its theological service of criticism and discernment. It is not a moral theology, simply judging the ethical value of actions, but a considered statement made in the light of the Scriptures read in the church, of the saving presence of God which it discerns and, in the light of that presence, it interprets the Scriptures. Hence it is really theology, for it is the *logos* of the *theos*, of God who is revealed salvifically in history and also in the concrete, political, strife-torn history of Latin America.

Translated by J. P. Donnelly

Biographical Notes

GERHARD ADLER was born in 1941. After studying humanities, he spent three years working on the German periodical *Herder-Korrespondenz*. Since 1970, he has been employed in radio (Südwestfunk) in Baden-Baden. Apart from articles and radio features, he has published *Revolutionäres Lateinamerika. Eine Dokumentation* (Paderborn, 1970); *Christlich—was heißt das?* (Düsseldorf, 1972), which he edited; *Die Jesus-Bewegung. Aufbruch der enttäuschten Jugend* (Düsseldorf, 1972); *Jesus People auf der Suche nach der "verlorenen Dimension". Eine Dokumentation mit Originaltonaufnahmen aus Kalifornien* (Freiburg, 1972)—a record.

CHRISTIAN DUQUOC O.P. was born on 22 December 1926 at Nantes and ordained in 1953. He studied at the Dominican Studium of Leysse (France), the University of Fribourg, the faculties of the Saulchoir (France) and the Biblical School of Jerusalem. A doctor of theology and with a diploma of the Biblical School of Jerusalem, he is professor of dogmatic theology at the Faculty of Theology of Lyons and is a member of the editorial committee of *Lumière et Vie*. His publications include *L'Église et le Progrès* and *Christologie,* I and II (Paris, 1972).

GUSTAVO GUTIÉRREZ-MERINO was born in Lima (Peru) on 8 June 1828. Licentiate in psychology at the University of Louvain (Belgium) and in theology at the University of Lyons (France), he is the national adviser to the Union of Catholic Students in Peru and teaches in the departments of theology and social science at the Catholic University of Lima. His publications include *La Pastoral de la Iglesia latinoamericana* (Montevideo, 1968) and *Apuntes para una Teología de la Liberación* (Lima, 1971).

LEANDER KECK, born in U.S.A. in 1928, is an ordained American Baptist. He pursued a theological education at Andover Newton Theological School, Kiel and Göttingen, Germany, and at Yale (Ph.D., 1957); his post-doctoral study was at Tübingen, Germany, and Cambridge, England. He has taught at Wellesley College and Vanderbilt University.

He is currently professor of New Testament and chairman of the Graduate School's Division of Religion at Emory University in Atlanta, Georgia. His publications include *A Future for the Historical Jesus* (Nashville, 1971 and London, 1972). He is editor of the "Lives of Jesus" series (Philadelphia and London) as well as the Monograph series of the Society of Biblical Literature.

NICHOLAS LASH was born in India in 1934 and was ordained in 1963. Master of Arts and Doctor of Philosophy of the University of Cambridge, where he is at present Fellow and Dean of St Edmund's House. Among his published works are *His Presence in the World* (London, 1968), *Authority in a Changing Church* (London, 1968), which he edited; *The Christian Priesthood*, edited with J. Rhymer (London, 1970); *Change in Focus* (London, 1973). He has also contributed articles to various reviews, including *Bijdragen, Downside Review, Heythrop Journal, History of Science, Irish Theological Quarterly, Istina, New Blackfriars and Tijdschrift voor Theologie.*

DIETER LÜHRMANN, who was born on 13 March 1939, studied theology from 1957 until 1962 in Bethel, Heidelberg and Göttingen, graduated in 1964 at Heidelberg, taught under G. Bornkamm from 1965 until 1968 at Heidelberg, since when he has taught New Testament studies there. His publications include *Das Offenbarungsverständnis bei Paulus und in den paulinischen Gemeinden* (1965) and *Die Redaktion der Logienquelle* (1968).

WALTER MAGASS was born in Gelsenkirchen in 1926. He studied theology and philosophy in Münster, Tübingen, Paris and Bonn. He edits and has contributed to *Linguistica Biblica*, the Bonn journal. He is a pastor in the Evangelical Church and has published, apart from essays on the semiotics of the parables in *Linguistica Biblica* (1970–1973), *Das öffentliche Schweigen. Antwort auf die Preisfrage der Deutschen Akademie für Sprache und Dichtung: Gibt es Maßstäbe für die Kunst der öffentlichen Rede in Deutschland* (Heidelberg, 1967); *Exempla ecclesiastica. Beispiele des apostolischen Marktverhaltens* (Bonn, 1972).

JOSEF NEUNER is a Jesuit priest. He was born in 1908 at Feldkirch, Austria, completed his studies with a doctorate at the Gregorian University in Rome, is teaching at the Papal Athenaeum in Poona (India) and was at the Vatican Council as a theologian. With H. Roos, he edited the doctrinal documents in German in *Der Glaube der Kirche* and in English in *The Teaching of the Catholic Church*, which has recently been completely reworked together with J. Dupuis under the title *The Christian Faith* (1973). With R. de Smet, he edited *Religious Hinduism*. He also edited the papers of the Bombay Seminar in *Christian Revelation and World Religions* and published other contributions to books and periodicals on theology, missiology and comparative religion.

RUDOLF PESCH was born at Bonn in 1936. He studied Catholic theology, history and German at the Universities of Bonn and Freiburg i.Br.;

doctor of philosophy (modern history, 1964), doctor of theology (New Testament, 1967); full lecturer in the department of New Testament studies at Innsbruck (1969); from 1971 onwards, he has been professor of Catholic theology with special reference to biblical studies in the department of religious studies at Frankfurt. He has published numerous works on the Bible, the most recent being *Jesu ureigene Taten? Ein Beitrag zur Wunderfrage* (Freiburg, 1970); *Freie Treue. Die Christen und die Ehescheidung* (Freiburg, 1971); *Der Besessene von Gerasa. Entstehung und Überlieferung einer Wundergeschichte* (Stuttgart, 1972) and *Die kleine Herde. Zur Theologie der Gemeinde* (Graz, 1973).

JUAN CARLOS SCANNONE was born in Buenos Aires in 1931, has been a Jesuit since 1949 and was ordained in 1962. He is a doctor of philosophy of Munich University and a licentiate in theology of Innsbruck University. At present he is Dean of the Faculty of Philosophy at the University of Buenos Aires (San Miguel), where he teaches the philosophy of theology. He is the vice-president of the Argentinian Society of Theology and an adviser to the review *Stromata*. His publications include *Sein und Inkarnation* (Freiburg and Munich, 1968) and numerous articles. On the freedom movement in Latin America, he has published "Hacia una dialéctica de la liberación", *Stromata*, 1 (1971); "La liberación latino-americana. Ontología del proceso auténticamente liberador," *ibid.*, 1-2 (1972); "Die Theologie der Befreiung in Lateinamerika", *Orientierung*, 1 (1973) (Spanish original: "La teología de la liberación". *Revista del CIAS*, 221, 1973); "Teólogia y política. El actual desafío planteado al lenguaje teológico latinoamericano de liberación", *Fe cristiana y cambio social en América Latina—Encuentro en El Escorial 1972* (Salamanca, 1973), summarized in "La théologie de la liberation en Amérique Latine", *Christus*, 75 (1972); "Situación de la problemática 'Fe y politica' en América Latina", *Fe y política* (Buenos Aires, 1973); "Transcendencia, praxis liberadora y lenguaje", *Nuevo mundo* (Buenos Aires), 5 (1973).

EDWARD SCHILLEBEECKX O.P. was born in Antwerp in 1914 and was ordained in 1941. He studied at the Dominican Faculty of Theology of the Saulchoir, at the École des Hautes Études and at the Sorbonne, Paris. Doctor of theology (1951) and master of theology (1959), he has been professor of dogmatic theology at the University of Nijmegen since 1958, and also visiting professor at Harvard University. He is also editor-in-chief of *Tijdschrift voor Theologie*. Among his published works are *Revelation and Theology, Concept of Truth and Theological Renewal, God and Man, World and Church, The Mission of the Church* and *God, the Future of Man*.